THE ROCK STARS
OF NEUROSCIENCE

To Duncan,
With deep gratitude
and friendship.
xo Faith

THE ROCK STARS OF NEUROSCIENCE

**HOW A GROUPIE IN CRISIS EMERGED AS THE HEROINE
OF HER FAMILY'S VICTORY OVER MENTAL ILLNESS**

A Memoir

F. D. Raphael

In memory of my beautiful mother, the epitome of courage, resilience, gratitude, and love.

Acknowledgements

Big love and gratitude to my husband of twenty-five years for your devotion and unwavering support. My sons –you are my heroes. Your fortitude continues to inspire me. I have loved you all my life.

Jennie Nash, my book coach, editor, and confidant, without whom this book would not exist. My sister, Dani Markman, your love supported me through writing each chapter. My brother, Sting, for finally inviting me to a MENSA dinner to meet your closest friends (who even approved my honorary MENSA membership). My wonderful father, for allowing me to turn your house into base camp, without any advance notice. My dear friend Nancy Farbman Cohen, who one day told me, "You ought to write a book;" she then read the entire first draft.

Andrew Solomon, for your inspiration as a brilliant author and journalist. Thank you for your encouraging words about my book. Dr. Adam Gazzaley, Dr. Michael Okun, Dr. Andrew Weil, and Dr. John Piacentini for your generous responses to being part of this story. Dr. Paul Shattuck for coming to our house for a burrito dinner, and sharing your insights about the profound social and economic issues facing emerging adults with autism.

For my friends whose unconditional love and support reminded me—in and out of crisis—that I was never alone. A special thanks to Stephanie Bronson, Charlotte "Cece" Mann, Carol Watkins, Gail Zappa, Rabbi Zoe Klein, and Cantor Evan Kent. Jeffrey Kramer, my great appreciation for your early advisement. You are my best friend I've never met. Tracey Yokas, and Laura Foti Cohen for your valuable editorial comments.

Elissa Henkin, Deborah Jacobowitz, and Michelle Bennett for your academic guidance—a gift far greater than words can express. My medical team for keeping me healthy: Dr. Kristi Funk, Dr. Eric Saslow, and Chris Mulligan. A very special thanks to Dr. Drew Schroeder, for a decade spent managing our family's care with empathy, compassion, and affection. I will always remember that day when you told me, "You're only as happy as your least happy child."

Contents

INTRODUCTION

E very life is a pilgrimage to understand the brain—its strengths and weaknesses, its delicate simplicity and rich complexity, its gentle benevolence or camouflaged malevolence. But in my life, this path has been the essence of everything. I was eight years old when my brain became sickened by cluster headaches—the beginning of my intimate involvement with the ways in which our brain can betray us.

I watched my brother's life-long suffering from the crushing combination of his MENSA brain crippled by undiagnosed Asperger's Syndrome (AS). Drug and alcohol addiction, a soul-sucking disease, contaminated my bosses' brains, the members of Aerosmith. Then my young sons both developed debilitating brain disorders—one had Tourette syndrome (TS), attention deficit disorder (ADD), and a mood disorder; and the other had obsessive-compulsive disorder (OCD), panic attacks, and depression.

In 2003, mental illness kidnapped me from a successful career in the music industry and dumped me into a dark, desolate abyss. I spiraled into a state of entropy in this unwelcoming landscape, haunted by years of inadequate prescription imperatives, orphan drugs to treat erratic and punishing symptoms of mental disease, and a spinning palette of psychiatrist and psychologist therapy sessions. My sons' conditions continued with little improvement.

Where are the experts? I wondered. I am not a doctor. I am a woman who needed help, a mother who needed to know as much as I could about how to fix a dysfunctional brain.

I found some answers through men who made brain science their life's work. From revered neurosurgeons to counter-culture heroes, my rock stars of neuroscience include Maharishi Mahesh Yogi, Dr. John C. Lilly, Dr. Simon Baron-Cohen, Dr. Dacher Keltner, Dr. Timothy Leary, Dr. Ross Greene, Dr. John Piacentini, Dr. Adam Gazzaley, Dr. Michael Okun, Dr. Andrew Weil, Dr. Michael Jenike, Dr. Lloyd Sederer, and Dr. Jon Kabat-Zinn. Each of these neuroscientists helped me through a kaleidoscope of mental health crises, most through personal relationships, several through their published work and articles, and in one instance, through a chance meeting in an airport in California.

Here are my notes, culled from more than a decade spent exploring and testing traditional and alternative therapies, cutting-edge technologies and surgeries, residential facilities, neuroelectrics, optogenetics, lead investigators for research grants and clinical trials. Consumed with finding the best treatment outcomes for my family, I became a groupie of neuroscientists.

In 2013, my transformation began. I understood that there are no experts, and there are no cures for mental illness. However, these rock stars gave me hope and bolstered my resilience. Against great odds, I pulled my family through this crisis, and we survived.

There are no maps or instructions to finding help for treating mental illness. This long-distance ride along treacherous roads filled with potholes and streets that go nowhere is like driving a snowmobile to Vegas. Yet, navigating this unwieldy terrain emboldened my advocacy.

Hope, often obscured by reason, requires a gigantic leap of faith; an action so powerful because all of the unknown possibilities exist in this infinite space. Hope is a choice to persevere, an opportunity to overcome improbable odds. We all possess undiscovered superhuman strengths. We can be transformed, and emerge from a crisis as heroes with death-defying courage, endurance, and love.

March 16, 2016
F. D. Raphael

*And those who were seen dancing were thought to
be insane by those who could not hear the music.*
—FRIEDRICH NIETZSCHE

CHAPTER 1

THE BLACK PLAINS...
MAHARISHI MAHESH YOGI

*I can't go back to yesterday because
I was a different person then.*
—ALICE IN LEWIS CARROLL'S *ALICE IN WONDERLAND*

The blood-curdling pain marked the moment a pattern was imprinted in my brain cells with permanent ink, an unforgettable memory, which was reinforced by the haunting anticipation of subsequent treacherous episodes. I was in the third grade when I experienced the first explosion of pain in my head, and by the time I turned twelve years old, the frequency and extraordinary incapacitation of these attacks required medical attention. They appeared without warning with a sudden *SMACK!* I'd sink into the nearest piece of furniture, petrified of moving or aggravating the already excruciating torment. My pediatrician ran numerous blood tests, and then made an appointment for me to see a neurologist. Apparently, I displayed no symptoms to identify a psychiatric disorder. After all, pre-teen anxiety and numerous other neurological conditions hadn't been invented yet, in 1968; thus, diagnosis and treatment were elusive.

Finally, my mother took me to see an *adolescent doctor*, an emerging field of physicians who saw patients transitioning from pediatrics to puberty. Dr. Jablonski was a young, hotshot doctor whose claim to fame, then, was that he delivered Jacqueline Kennedy's premature baby son— unfortunately, the boy died less than a week later. A personal thank you note to the young pediatrician from Mrs. Kennedy hung on the wall next to his Yale Medical School diploma and board certification from the Commonwealth of Massachusetts.

Dr. Jablonski suggested the headaches might be symptomatic of an allergic reaction, although I was not a kid prone to allergies. At sleep-away camp, girls in my bunk would dare me to wash my hands with poison ivy leaves. I never got a rash and at seventy-five cents a dare, I made over six dollars by the end of summer. Nonetheless, Dr. J. prescribed a bitter-tasting liquid antihistamine, which had no influence whatsoever on the headaches. The only way I survived these intermittent, yet diabolical sledgehammers inside my brain was through the extraordinary discovery of something I called *the black plains*.

It was the last week of summer break, before eighth grade would commence. The weather had been particularly humid all summer in South Middlesex County and on August 25, 1969, the temperature soared to ninety-three degrees Fahrenheit. By late afternoon, it had cooled down enough for me to go outside and pick raspberries from my father's berry bramble in the backyard. He also grew blackberries and strawberries, but the bright-fuchsia raspberries were in a league of their own, as was my mother's homemade raspberry jam. In fact, the counselors at my summer camp used to beg me to ask my mom to bring a jar whenever my father and she came to visit for Parents' Day.

Raspberry picking is an acquired skill. It takes time and experience to identify the perfect berry. Observation is key. A berry's ripeness is determined by its size, scent, color, and feel. The sweetest berries from the bramble were always large and firm—not even a little bit squishy. I would roll the raspberry fuzz between my thumb and index finger until the berry released with a gentle wiggle and dropped into my basket. If you look closely, a raspberry is a cluster of seeds. Each little seed has a hook provided by nature to help that seed grab onto something passing by and carry it to where it can drop off and grow into new raspberries.

"Pick the nice, big ones," Dad had always instructed in his most authoritative voice. I had to earn my father's trust before he'd allow me in his garden, before I could actually touch his precious *lovies*. "Look at them first. Find a section where the berries are uniform in color and firm to the touch. Very gentle-like, twist them from the white pulp. The ripe ones fall right off."

That late August afternoon, nearing the end of the berry-picking season, my father made sure I was paying close attention. "The berries that feel like you have to pull at them aren't ready," he added. "Just leave them alone." I eagerly nodded my head in agreement.

As I bent down to reach for a cluster of berries, I was stunned by a sharp jolt shooting from behind my eye towards the front of my head. Perspiration collected along my hairline and the back of my neck. The air was warm and heavy, like dog's breath. Before I could recover, another painful shock followed. I pressed my fingers into my right eyelid to try to contain the pain, but the sensation was so excruciating that it impeded my breathing. I gasped as more shocks fired through my skull in rapid succession. My heart was thumping fast, as each breath I attempted tugged at my throbbing temple. I had no time to waste, no time to explain anything to anyone because the pain was chasing me. *"Quick. Just run inside, get to bed!"* a voice told me. My lumbering body felt heavy; the pores on my skin oozed with sweat and my legs moved slowly, like I was pulling them out of molasses. I didn't call for help because at this point, these episodes had long been a common annoyance to my mother, and all my father would have done was send me to her.

I finally made it to my room and toppled onto my bed, my head weighing a ton as it crashed into my pillow. The palpitation on the right side of my face raced, a pulsating staccato drowned out by the relentless drilling behind my right eye. Capillaries stretched taut behind my skull like a boa constrictor. My right arm dangled limply off the side of the bed. I continued squeezing my pillow, as each contraction seemed to cut the blood supply in my cranium. My eyes were closed as I slipped in and out of consciousness, barely aware that my sense of being was disintegrating. My body numbed. Then my bed began twirling, spinning in circles that grew wider and wider, smoother with each rotation, a sensation similar to when a plane reaches altitude and it feels as if you aren't even moving. I had no idea how this was happening. My brain had already surrendered to the formidable pain.

Gravity seemed to lose its hold on me as I sensed a presence lean over and lift me from my bed. Without touching me, a force swiftly moved me to a faraway place. This was something new but I wasn't afraid. Minutes, or hours, might have passed until all movement halted. I had arrived at my destination. I remember wondering whether I should open my eyes, or if I could. Thoughts began to collide as my mind released into *the black plains*. *The plains* wasn't a scary place. I came up with the name because that's what I saw in my altered state of consciousness. Somehow, when I transcended the apex of my intolerable agony, I didn't die. Instead, I ended up in a place that was simply black, vast, and flat, two-dimensional. Still on my bed, I saw myself in this place. I looked calm and content in *the plains*, appearing translucent, like clouds wafting across the western sky. I was meant to be there.

I was alive, and for an as-yet-unknown reason, *the black plains* was an essential part of my being. While floating, I was carefully brought back to my bedroom and placed on my bed, without anyone or anything actually holding my body. I had no idea how long I'd been away in that state until I saw the time on the clock on my bedside table. Whatever took me to *the plains* brought me back the next morning. I heard my family in the kitchen eating breakfast and felt relieved to know that nothing bad had happened to them while I was away.

The black plains became my sanctuary, a place free from agony. Between the fever that came with the headaches and the diminished breathing the pain imposed, I could have suffocated, but instead I reached those *plains*. At first, I thought it was just a dream, a happy conclusion to a painful episode. I attempted to describe *the plains* to my sister, Dani, who was five years younger. She simply rolled her eyes and walked away to watch TV. No one understood what was happening to me, but I was aware that something in my brain wasn't right, and that my experience on August 25 was far from normal.

By my senior year of high school, I had been experiencing an increase in frequency and pain escalation from what was finally diagnosed as "cluster headaches." I later learned that cluster headaches (CH) occur in attacks, with pain usually emanating from one side of the head, around the eye, in the temple, or any combination of those areas. The pain from this condition is considered to be remarkably more painful than a severe migraine, and so devastating in its intensity that some sufferers experience suicidal thoughts during an attack. As a result, according to University of Vermont, College of Medicine, neurology professor Robert Shapiro, cluster headaches have been colloquially named "suicide headaches." Sometimes I got to *the black plains*, where relief awaited me, but not always. It wasn't entirely in my control.

My headaches became as time-consuming as any after-school activity; I went home sick twelve days during my last year of high school.

I decided that the headaches were some sort of punishment because they distanced me from what I needed most: my mother's compassion and empathy. I'd approach her, pleading for help as the pallor of my face changed from shades of olive-brown to greenish-white, and the sweat mounting behind my ears forced my glasses to slide down my face. My hair was matted, dark-brown curls sticking to my hairline like clumps of fusilli pasta. My mother would then usually place the back of her hand on my forehead.

"You feel warm and clammy," she'd say with a grimace after touching my wet skin. Then came the obligatory solution: "Go lie down and I'll get you some aspirin." She'd return to my bedroom seconds later with two pills and a glass of cold water and hand me a cool cloth to place over my eyes.

"Do you want me to wake you for dinner?" she'd offer.

"No," I'd answer. "I'll get up if I'm feeling better."

I spent many nights crying myself to sleep until not a sound, not a whimper revealed that I was alive, except for the involuntary trickle of tears that dripped off my face the way water leaks from an old faucet. The only witnesses to my suffering were the discolored stains on the wooden floor in my bedroom. My door was closed as the late afternoon sun turned to dusk, then darkness, and then morning. Usually, I'd go to school the next day without remark.

My parents tolerated pain and physical suffering with an even disposition, as though negative experiences were essential to appreciating positive ones. When I was a teenage girl, my parents—especially my mother—behaved with unflinching determination, consistently and optimistically exhibiting the epitome of endurance. "Tomorrow will be a new day," she'd always say. "How could we appreciate the good days, if we didn't experience bad ones?" A good night's sleep and two aspirin, or Alka-Seltzer tablets, were the panacea for colds, the flu, fever, headaches, stomachaches—every common symptom of the human condition. I was on my own with my headaches because my reality wasn't the same as my mother's. She simply couldn't understand the depth of my misery.

What's in our heads reflects how we perceive reality, and being sick made me feel like my soul was leaving me. Chronic pain is debilitating and then it sucks you like a vacuum into depression, where suffering is even more heinous because we are conscious of the isolation it imposes. Depression is especially divisive because we cannot see or feel another's pain, making the hurt seem lesser on the outside than it actually is. I wanted my mother to think that I was brave, to appreciate my valiant effort to cope with this crushing affliction. Instead, I think she perceived my low tolerance to pain as a weakness. This became a literal and philosophical point of departure between my parents and me. I knew that I couldn't live the rest of my life fearful about the next onslaught of crippling torture, but I understood that their ability to help me was limited. We had exhausted the varied treatments that Western medicine could provide: drug prescriptions containing opioids, benzodiazepines—all which I would later learn were highly addictive—beta-blocker prophylactics that caused weight gain, and no one really understood how they worked to prevent headaches anyway.

Then one afternoon, driving to the Stop & Shop, I spotted a white clapboard house with a sign reading TRANSCENDENTAL MEDITATION on the other side of Route 9. After a brief discussion, my parents offered to pay for me to learn how to meditate.

"If it can help with those damn headaches, it will be well worth the money," my dad believed. The only condition was that my mother, clearly uncomfortable with me "engaging in this hippie stuff," insisted on coming to the introductory class, which I appreciated. I called the number from the sign and booked my sessions.

From 1958 to 1968 the Maharishi Mahesh Yogi embarked on five world tours to spread the teaching of transcendental meditation. *Maharishi* is from the ancient Sanskrit language of India's Hinduism, Buddhism, Sikhism, and Jainism scriptures. It is an exalted name meaning "Great Seer." He is reported to have trained more than 40,000 teachers, who in turn have taught the Transcendental Meditation technique to more than five million people. In the 1970s, the Maharishi founded the Students' International Meditation Society, SIMS, with centers at Yale, Harvard, and UCLA. The mass adoption and scientific research of this centuries-old practice had legitimately provided a new field of neuroscience, with proven benefits for reducing stress, anxiety, and pain.

The day of my first session, we arrived at a former residential split-level house surrounded by an abandoned parking lot. My mom and I stood on the concrete doorstep for several minutes. There wasn't a doorbell or note indicating that we were expected. Questioning what to do next, I looked at my mother and shrugged my shoulders. "Why not?" I said, turning the front doorknob and finding it unlocked. We stepped into the foyer with a dilapidated wooden floor, buckled slats, and chunks of plaster missing from its ceiling. Though this house was situated just off Route 9, a major road congested with traffic, as soon as we closed the front door behind us we could hear nothing from outside. The quiet this house commanded was prepossessing.

"Pretty grimy," my mother whispered as she continued her inspection of the box-shaped room.

"Yeah," I agreed, though *skanky* was the word I would have used. I think we spoke in hushed tones to each other because once inside the tacky façade, we were clearly caught up in something unfamiliar, something greater than us. There was no office signage in this hall, only a closed door in front of us.

"Is this the waiting room?" my mother asked, pointing to the stack of folded metal chairs on the floor. We noticed a small ledge on one of the walls, on top of which sat a cheap glass vase, seven inches tall, and cloudy with gummy fingerprints. It contained several pens, which I figured were for writing a check before the session.

I proceeded to pry open two brown metal chairs in an effort to appear as though I knew what I was doing. The door in front of us was closed, taunting us like Pandora's Box.

"Are you supposed to wait here for your *Mareshishi*, or whatever his name is?"

"I guess so," I said, preoccupied with my chair, which bobbled back and forth against the uneven floor. I figured that if nothing else, the clattering sound would surely get someone's attention.

Ten minutes later, my Indian guide slid his lanky body though the barely open door then sealed it closed behind him. An overwhelming musky scent of burning incense seeped into the waiting room. He walked towards us with measured footing, not saying a word until his feet practically touched the legs of our chairs. Introducing himself as Teacher, he spoke in a soft monotone, explaining to us that this was a supremely spiritual experience, one that required my commitment. I solemnly agreed. Without leaving her chair, my mother handed my teacher a check for five sessions. Teacher motioned for me to advance to the door, then arched his arm over my head as he pressed it open. He closed the door behind us, which was a good thing because I knew if I glanced back at my mother's expression, I would have crumbled with laughter.

The only artifacts in this deceptively large room were plastic flowers in a green-colored, cracked plastic pot placed below a framed, lopsided poster of the Maharishi Mahesh Yogi. The linoleum tile was pitted with scuffmarks and chips. Teacher looked more like he had been living on the streets than someone about to bring me closer to the light.

His shoulder-length hair looked unkempt: parted in the middle and greasy, thick strands of gray and black hair hung straight, except for a small patch of rigid waves, like someone used a crimping iron just on that section. He wore a dingy brown polyester Nehru jacket, white linen pants, and brown sandals. His voice was so small I could barely hear him. His near-black-colored eyes didn't seem to have pupils, and making eye contact was like staring into large black buttons. He instructed me to sit facing him on the floor and then waited for me to negotiate a comfortable position. My legs were folded over each other, pretzel-shaped, my arms rested on my thighs, my palms on my knees. Teacher had to help me position my hands correctly.

"Like *dees*," he said in his soft accent as he turned my wrists open, facing the ceiling. His grip was surprisingly strong. "You *alvays* meditate *vith* your palms open fully."

Okay, so I'm not Flexie the Pocket Monkey, I thought to myself.

"Now I *vill* give you your mantra," he began. "This is a *verd* chosen only for you. You must never give it away." He leaned towards me. "Close your eyes."

With my eyes shut, he clapped his hands so close to my face that I felt the air between us, and he spoke one word. I immediately understood it to be a gift. To this day, I've never told anyone my mantra. Teacher and I chanted the word together until I said it correctly. Every meditation would begin by us repeating my mantra out loud, together. Then, I'd repeat it silently, over and over.

I soon began to relax, mesmerized by his command of *stillness*. Suddenly this man, who some might call a charlatan, seemed to embody a supernatural wisdom. I became an attentive student. I watched him when his eyes were closed and I recognized peacefulness. He was in control of his being and part of every molecule in the universe. I only sensed that connection because I didn't yet have the experience of it. I was still on the outside looking in, but I wanted what he was offering. I wanted that transcendence of self.

By my third session, I closed my eyes, sat in front of Teacher, and allowed his voice to enter my consciousness. This time, I experienced a very deep meditation, which took me beyond my physical body to a place of just being, with intermittent moments of heightened consciousness. My body tingled with warmth as my mind became a blank slate, *tabula rasa*. Gone were the typical crazy narratives and incomplete thoughts that would often collapse like awkward somersaults in my crowded mind.

Twenty minutes later, Teacher's voice, which now sounded clear and strong, called me back to the present. I felt strange and surprised, like I had been caught falling asleep in class. I looked at Teacher and for the first time, I smiled at him. My cheeks flushed, knowing that I'd made it to this new place of enlightenment. Meditation pioneer Dr. Deepak Chopra calls these moments "the gap"—*pure consciousness*. My brain expanded to allow ample space for my thoughts. My body felt cozy and my skin seemed to fit just right. Only Teacher knew about my secret place because he'd guided me there, and I felt immense gratitude to him—the first rock star of neuroscience I ever encountered.

I would come to learn that meditation wasn't quite as easy as it had seemed that afternoon, and that altering my brain was going to be a lifelong pursuit. It would take a lot of practice before I could return to that place, before I could exert some distance and control over my pain. But in the shabby house with that odd guide, I learned the first essential lesson: we do not have to settle for one mode of perception. We do not have to accept what our brains first offer us.

CHAPTER 2

UNTIL TOMORROW COMES...
DR. SIMON BARON-COHEN

*I think madness can be an escape. If things are not too
good, you maybe want to imagine something better.*
—JOHN FORBES NASH, JR.

A brain is like a snowflake, each one delicate and compact, uniquely deliberate in its design. I was five years old when I recognized that my brother's brain was quite different from mine. A fresh snow had fallen in Boston, and the late morning sky emitted powerful beams of sunlight. Our mom got us ready to play outside in the cold and zipped us up in our bulky snowsuits as we stomped our feet into our boots. Mom knitted us each our own pair of mittens that were clipped to our jackets so they wouldn't get lost; yellow ones for me, blue for my brother.

Bursting with excitement to make my first snow angel of the year, I pushed my seven-year-old brother, Sting, out the front screen door. The fresh, crisp air against my face felt invigorating as I pulled on Sting's jacket for him to follow me into the snowdrift in the front yard. Sting just sat on the snow, refusing to lie down and flap his wings with me. Instead, he gazed out towards the sky, squinting at the white brightness surrounding us. When I looked at him, he seemed so far away from me. The sunlight glistened against his alabaster skin, while the reflection of the snow crystals twinkled against the golden specs of color in his brown eyes. In that moment, he seemed temporal, like he was part of another world.

"C'mon," I insisted as I pulled him down into the snow beside me.

He had a look of great consternation; his furrowed eyebrows were visible below the hood of his jacket. I laughed and although he tried to force a smile, I sensed something he didn't communicate: he was angry, extremely angry, with me.

"Sting, you'll have fun making a snow angel," I said. "Just move your arms really big up and down so you can have wings, like this." I demonstrated, scraping my jacket against the snow, high above my head. The only audible sound was my waterproof pants crunching against the snow to complete the bottom of my sculpture.

"I don't like this," he stated, lying on his back, looking at the sky. Either he didn't understand me or maybe he couldn't coordinate the movements of his arms and legs scooping into the crusty, white drifts. My brother remained completely still for a few seconds before sitting upright with his legs crossed in a seemingly random gesture. For the next several moments I watched him rock back and forth with a trance-like urgency. He was alert but somewhere else, drawn to another place in his mind until, without warning, he stood up and abandoned me.

"Mum told you to stay with me!" I called out to him as he went into the house without saying another word.

I didn't understand what had happened, but I was angry at Sting because he never wanted to play with me. He was supposed to watch over me. Now I'd have to go inside, too. My mother was upset because it had taken her a lot of time to get us dressed in our snowsuits and she believed that, whenever possible, children should play outside. Seconds later, two neighborhood kids, Steve and Jay, walked up to our front door and asked Sting if he wanted to build an igloo. With very little fanfare, my mother sent him back outside. I, however, remained in the house, and my mother unzipped my snowsuit. Sadly, I removed my boots and threw them back in the closet.

"Do you have a shovel we can use?" Jay asked, standing outside the screen door.

Sting didn't respond, so my mother answered. "Of course," she smiled warmly. "It's over by the garage." Then she looked at my brother. "Go with Jay and get the shovel."

"Come on, let's go!" Jay, two years older than Sting, was a charismatic leader.

Sting showed the boys where the shovel was then handed it to Steve, in a gesture that looked as though he was done with his assignment. He followed the boys to our front yard, and as they began gregariously scooping up piles of snow, Sting barely engaged. He just continued to stand behind and observe them. Finally, Steve managed to involve Sting, and soon my brother was making his first igloo. As I watched this pantomime from our dining room window, I wished that I could have played with them. It looked like so much fun; but my mother had other plans for me. She called me into the kitchen and handed me an apron and the wooden spoon, which meant that she and I would be making Jell-O!

Less than an hour later Sting came back into the house, but didn't invite the boys inside. He took off his mittens and outer clothes, then headed for his sanctuary: his bedroom. Sting didn't like playing with anyone as much as he enjoyed being alone in his bedroom with the door closed. At first I thought it was only me he disliked playing with, but I saw that this extended to kids his own age, too. Even as a child, I remember thinking it was strange that Sting didn't seem to like playing with anyone else at all.

I had that same feeling about Sting being different when something happened a few summers later, after I returned from a six-week stay at sleep-away camp in New Hampshire. Sting was going to a day camp in Natick, Massachusetts, and Monday through Friday the bus picked him up in the morning and brought him home in the afternoon. The day after I got home, we had a storm—rain, wind, and thunder, and Sting didn't come home at three o'clock like he usually did. By three thirty, my mother had called the camp. After hanging up the phone, she handed me my rain jacket and told me to get in the car.

"They don't know where your brother is," she said.

My mother drove the same route as the bus, heading towards camp, while I stared out the window in the front seat, looking for a yellow rain jacket through the downpour. The car windows were foggy but after a few minutes, I saw him standing under the concrete covering on a roundabout ramp not far from camp. Sting was 10 years old but looked much smaller, his figure pummeled by the force of the storm. My mother's teeth remained clenched tight and I knew she was frightened because her face was like stone, barely revealing any emotion as she pulled over to the side of the road where Sting was standing.

"Get in the car, now!" she called out the window to him over the clatter of the rain. "What are you doing here?"

He waved at us, a delayed reaction to the fact that the car had already stopped right next to him. He stepped off the curb and while one sneaker made it into the car, the other was submerged in a swirling pool of fast-moving water. Clumsily, he tripped into the seat behind me.

"Why weren't you on the bus?" my mother demanded. "No one at camp knew where to find you!"

The rubber from his raincoat refused to yield to the leather on the car seat. He was nearly strangled by his rain jacket bunching up before he could twist it around his upper body. He told us that these three bullies were chasing him during camp bus line-up. "So I just kept running away from them," he exclaimed with frustration. "When I stopped, the stupid bus drove away without me!" Cold, tired, and disoriented, Sting figured he'd just walk home; but camp was almost five miles from our house. He had walked half a mile, the wind whipping against his bare legs, as each passing car sprayed him with puddles of water. He was soaking wet, but couldn't walk any further, so he stopped at the roundabout.

As he told this story, shivering in the back seat of the car, I kept my face pressed against the cool window. My tears trickled down to the bottom of the glass. Why did horrible things always seem to happen to Sting? Why was my mother always so anxious about him? I felt confused and that uneasy feeling returned, reminding me that something wasn't right. I loved my brother, but I didn't understand him. There was a kind of innocence and fragility about Sting, a sense that at any moment calamity could strike and my brother would be gone, or worse, left for dead.

When Sting was in junior high school, a pattern emerged. Sting became a lot like a little professor, his brain containing a compendium of information about topics that wouldn't interest most 13-year-old kids, such as aphids and plant fungicides. This made him a target, and Sting didn't have any friends to deflect attention from the kids who pestered him.

A school counselor referred my parents to a Boston University psychology professor known for his research with teens with delayed social behavior. After three sessions with this man, Sting spent two consecutive Saturdays undergoing diagnostic tests and assessments. My brother's IQ performance revealed genius level in the range of the top 2 percent of the population, which made him qualified to join an international organization of similar brainiacs called MENSA.

The psychologist concluded that my brother should join MENSA as a social outlet so that he could be around people with whom he could share the intensity of his knowledge and interests. So when my dad drove Sting to a MENSA meeting at a member's house in Sudbury, the town next to ours, we all felt slightly encouraged that this might be a positive social experience for him. Sting was dressed in his fancy clothes—a brown herringbone jacket, brown corduroys, loafers, a nice shirt, and my dad helped him with his brown and blue striped clip-on tie.

I was already waiting at the door when they got home an hour later.

"I don't think I'll go back," Sting stated, without expressing any emotions about an event that I had imagined would be an exciting new opportunity. My father followed Sting into the house. He looked disappointed and sad. Dad explained that Sting was the only kid there amongst a handful of adults who had no interest engaging with a kid in junior high school.

"Perhaps MENSA is something your son may want to pursue later in life," the BU psychologist suggested to my parents. He told them to keep Sting involved in activities and hobbies, and that he would most likely grow out of "it"—meaning his emotional disconnect with others, which by now had become disruptive in nature and further sequestered him from being understood.

Sting's voice had changed during puberty—but that wasn't the only development causing him to sound different. Quite randomly, he would repeat words in a strange cadence, sounding more like a cartoon, sort of like Bart Simpson.

"Jiffy Looobe, Jiffy Looobe," he'd squeal as his body started rocking back and forth, his left leg several inches behind his right—an action my father called "shuckling." When Sting was really excited about a thought he'd shuckle faster and faster, rocking on his left leg, then onto his right, increasing the rhythm of his movements as he'd rub his hands together, somehow able to maintain his balance. He'd suddenly lock into these thoughts—in class, around family, in the midst of conversations—a behavior so bizarre that it was both frightening and humiliating. His mind would be somewhere far away, oblivious to the attention he attracted.

My parents thought a change might be good for us all. They bought a new house and we moved to the other side of town, where my brother could attend the other public high school. We could all have a fresh start. At the time, my sister and I thought we were moving because we needed a bigger house—one with stairs, we hoped, and big enough so we could each have our own bedroom. There wasn't anything new to talk about regarding my brother, so we rarely did. As he matured, his social awkwardness became more obvious. He didn't know how to make friendships and continued to be an accessible mark for bullies.

Unfortunately, the guilt and alienation of constantly avoiding the elephant in the room brought out the worst in all of us. Unknowingly, Sting had become a vacuum in every conversation, sucking in the rich dynamics of discourse with endless monologues and factoids about his interests, unaware of the irrelevance of his contributions. It was easy to become disinterested in what Sting had to say, which further alienated him from others.

For example, my parents hosted the annual Thanksgiving dinner, which I loved because it was an opportunity to be with most of my aunts, uncles, and eight cousins, some of whom we only saw several times a year. As was typical, our aunts and uncles would ask us all about school.

One year, Aunt Lana greeted Sting with a warm hug and asked, "How are you, honey? Tell me what's new."

Not great with names, Sting smiled and replied, "Fine, Aunt Jane," and went on to ask her about her new Mercedes.

"Sting," I interrupted in a quiet voice, "that's Aunt Lana, not Aunt Jane, remember?"

He ignored me and spoke over my mild admonition. "It's a real beauty and all, but do you know how many miles it gets to the gallon?" he asked Aunt Lana.

She only stammered, trying to respond.

"Nevertheless," Sting said, not waiting for her response, "it's a real gas guzzler."

Throughout dinner, he continued talking about large foreign cars and gasoline inefficiency, companies that made various car parts, and why the system design had been altered. Sting was always on the alert for an awkward segue to continue talking about this topic, always speaking over the din of dinner conversation to maintain control of the dialog. Often, he didn't seem to notice when people would walk away from him mid-conversation. My mother got in the habit of trying to offer Sting social cues, like whispering, "Okay, that's enough, give someone else a chance to talk," or sometimes she'd place her index finger over her lips.

Sting didn't understand the redirects, which resulted in more uncomfortable social experiences. When I would invite friends over, I'd make Sting promise to stay in his room. I tried to make him as invisible as I could. He did, however, stand his ground, and nicknamed me "Dodo," as in Dodo bird, his way of telling me he wished I would become extinct.

My brother and I never spoke to one another in school and if we passed each other in the hallway, I acted as though I didn't know him. I was a freshman in high school and Sting was a junior. On one particular morning, after the bell rang, my teacher kept our homeroom door open. All was quiet until I heard my brother's lone voice bouncing off the metal lockers in the empty hallway: "HELP! SOMEONE! GET AWAY FROM ME!" Sting's cries echoed down the hall and seemed to stop just outside my door. Next came the sounds of hard-covered books slamming into metal, and then falling to the ground, as if they had been the battered victims of a tug-of-war. Without even knowing the reason for his distress, I became instantly mortified. I sank down in my chair and pretended to review my homework, burying my head in my book. I wasn't sure who in the class knew that Sting was my brother, but acknowledging our relationship certainly wasn't the way to fast-track my popularity.

Eventually a teacher got involved and sent my brother and the bullies who spit yellow phlegm on his face and shirt to the principal's office. These kinds of incidents had plagued my brother since childhood, and were an ongoing cause of heightened fear, anxiety, and anger for him. This time, Sting swiped back at one of the kids who had been pushing him against the lockers and inadvertently scratched his eye. My brother had blood on his fingernail and the thug had blood on his face, so the extent of the bleeding or to whom it belonged was unclear.

Principal Rigopoulos was a calm, soft-spoken man, and the tallest adult in the building—he could almost literally see everything. He liked Sting and displayed great empathy towards him, usually calling my mother and describing the where and when of a given altercation. He'd try to explain to Sting and my mother that when Sting would scream for help and call these bullies names they didn't understand—like "dunderheads"—it only made them laugh, further igniting a volatile situation. The principal suggested that these bullies actually enjoyed watching Sting unravel and lose control.

"If he could just walk away or remain calm," the principal suggested, "they'd leave him alone."

If only Sting could be calm when being jostled against metal lockers or spit on like a wild monkey. If only he could walk away so that people wouldn't notice him biting his own hand to hold back his anger. If only he could control his rocking back and forth to find respite in his mind.

It's easier to suggest walking away when it isn't happening to you.

This time, Mr. Rigopoulos thought it best for my brother to have lunch in his office for the duration of high school, and Sting appreciated that arrangement.

It wasn't long before I received my share of ridicule for being the sister of a "retard," a common word back then, but still just as loathsome. These punks didn't know that my brother was a genius, a card-carrying MENSA member in possession of an extraordinary ability to recall information. We would later learn that Sting had hyperthymesia, a rare condition where people exhibit an ability to recall specific, detailed information from their past without relying on any mnemonic strategies or cues. If someone today randomly raised the topic of oil prices in the 1980s, Sting's brain could immediately retrieve the OPEC oil prices per barrel from 1980 to 1989 and the impact the oil cartel had on fluctuating dollar costs at the pump. He could even remember the daily price for a gallon of gasoline at Smitty's gas station, near our house.

In 1988, I lived in my parents' home for several months. At the time I was 30, and making plans to get married and move to California. My sister, Dani, had just finished her season singing with the Pittsburgh Opera Company and was home, too. As we got older my sister, mother, and I thoroughly enjoyed each other's company and often made plans together. One evening, we went to see the movie *Rain Man* starring Tom Cruise and Dustin Hoffman. During the 1989 Oscars, the film won awards for Best Picture, Best Original Screenplay, Best Director, and Best Actor in a Leading Role for Hoffman. At that time, it was the go-to film to see in the theaters. *Rain Man* is a comedy-drama about two brothers, a yuppie and an autistic savant named Raymond, who didn't know each other until their father died and left behind a lucrative estate. The character

Raymond (Rain Man) was based on the life of Kim Peek, a mega savant from Utah.

Approximately fifteen minutes into the film, we each saw something terrifyingly familiar: my brother, then 33 years old, was more like Raymond than anyone else we had ever seen before. The thing that made Sting different had a name now, and all at once our collective tears erupted, years of repressed pressure in a volcanic release of relief and despair. Here was our brother on screen, and here was what was wrong with him. Throughout the film, I remember laughing almost uncontrollably during the funny scenes and crying hysterically during the poignant ones. I could barely look at my mother, who'd spent decades under the scrutiny of in-laws, cousins, and even friends, who judged her for how she raised her son.

Why can't she make him normal? they'd wonder.

The theatre had sold out and when the movie was over, we stayed in our seats until we were the only people remaining. In that moment, I could feel my mother's aching heart as it deflated with self-blame and guilt, her chest sinking as the oxygen slowly seeped out. The tissue around the muscle shriveled up and all that remained was a gaping hole. I wept for my mother whose heart, throughout the vicissitudes in life, had always been full of love.

My sister broke the silence. "Dustin Hoffman was incredible," she said. "He sounded just like Sting—it was amazing. Sting isn't as bad, but maybe he's a savant, too? Now we can explain his problems to a doctor, right?"

Sting was much more high-functioning than Raymond. He lived alone in a condominium he'd bought after he graduated from Boston College. He self-published a book about the 1980s energy crisis called *King Energy*. But it was Sting's social awkwardness, the colorless pitch to his voice, his one-track mind, and his peculiar gesticulations when he was "in his mind" that were so clearly recognizable and accentuated in Raymond.

With her head down to hide her tears, my mother grabbed my hand with her left and my sister's hand with her right. "Maybe, maybe," she muttered. What she didn't say was, *"Why now, after 33 years of not knowing, of everyone telling me he'd grow out of it?"*

Asperger's syndrome (AS) was first described in Germany in 1944, but it would take another 50 years before AS would have the research and diagnostic criteria to be published in the *Diagnostic and Statistical Manual of Mental Disorders (DSM)*, the bible of psychiatric diagnoses, published by the American Psychiatric Association. These diagnostic codes are universal, and adhered to by physicians and insurance companies. According to the *DSM-4*, published in 1994, the symptoms of Asperger's syndrome are as follows:

> *"Significant difficulty in nonverbal behaviors such as the lack of eye contact, few facial expressions, awkward body postures. Failure to develop friendships with other children of the same age. Repetitive patterns of behavior, interests, and activities with one or two topics, that is abnormal either in intensity, subject, or focus; and which become an all-encompassing preoccupation."*

Reading this apt description of Sting written by psychiatrists, neuroscientists, and other people who never met my brother was almost hurtful. In this clinical assessment, the authors seemed to know my brother better than anyone in his life did.

Over the next several years, I collected articles about Sting's disorder. In 2009, I discovered my rock star of AS and high-functioning autism, Dr. Simon Baron-Cohen, cousin of the infamous actor Sasha, who had written an editorial in the *New York Times* entitled "The Short Life of a Diagnosis." This superb article best explains the decision-making process behind how a mental disorder is determined and then published in the *DSM*. In the case of AS, after publication of the *DSM-4*, there had been much debate about its relationship to autism, and whether or not it should remain a unique diagnostic code or fall under the autism spectrum.

Baron-Cohen writes, "*A classification system that can be changed so freely and so frequently can't be close to following Plato's recommendation of 'carving nature at its joints.'*" There are few psychiatric categories with a clear molecular component, such as Down syndrome or Fragile X, which can be identified by a blood test. Dr. Baron-Cohen's team published the first candidate gene study, which identified 14 genes associated with AS. However, his concern in this editorial is that there hadn't been enough research to determine if AS and classic Autism are genetically identical or distinct.

In the revised *DSM-5* published in 2013, a new generation of psychiatrists and researchers determined that Asperger's syndrome and Autism Spectrum Disorders (ASD) exist under the same diagnostic code, with the only difference being the severity of symptoms. The obvious similarities between the two disorders involve problems with social interaction, having very niche interests, and difficulty handling emotions, while the fundamental difference is that those with Asperger's syndrome tend to display good intelligence and language acquisition. One of the most problematic aspects of reclassification is ensuring that the patient receives appropriate treatment no matter where they fall on the spectrum.

Diagnostic codes have far-reaching influence, and understanding the criteria in the *DSM* is essential. Distilling universally accepted insights in a very subjective and temporal snapshot culled from the largest net cast, the *DSM* gathers the data of symptomology of psychiatric and neurological disorders and considers the economic and social impact of the diagnostic code in its re-classification. The book is intermittently updated, and some mental illnesses that were included in a previous version of the *DSM* have been eliminated; some new illnesses will emerge or be re-categorized. Years later, I would confront the *DSM*'s power to delay my own son's diagnosis and how it would impact his access to treatment.

Dr. Baron-Cohen is a cognitive neuroscientist, Professor of Developmental Psychopathology, University of Cambridge and Fellow at Trinity College, and Director, Autism Research Centre (ARC) in Cambridge, England. Not surprisingly, Baron-Cohen received a Lifetime Achievement Award from MENSA. During an interview with the organization Autism Speaks, Baron-Cohen discussed how, in 1999, his team opened one of the first clinics for the diagnosis and support of adults with Asperger's syndrome, "for the lost generation of people born before 1994, when Asperger's syndrome was first recognized in the English-speaking medical world."

Sting was part of this "lost generation," and I wished that I had known about Dr. Baron-Cohen back then. Since hearing him speak, and reading several of his studies and his book *Autism and Asperger Syndrome: The Facts*, it became obvious to me that Dr. Baron-Cohen understood my brother's brain. He knew the suffering my brother had endured as a result of living a life without a diagnosis. I, on the other hand, had spent nearly 35 years not knowing my own brother, not understanding his odd disaffection. Sting couldn't act normal because his brain wasn't normal, and for more than three decades our family and society tried to stuff him into the normal box, which continually rejected him.

My parents, meanwhile, pined for Sting's stolen life. There are those who believe that as soon as you attach a name to something, that's what one becomes, while others believe that a rose by any other name is still a rose. I, however, am an advocate for early diagnosis because with intervention and appropriate treatment, Aspies—the colloquial name for those with the syndrome—can and do lead rich, full lives.

I don't understand how parents can allow fear of a diagnosis to sabotage their family's chance for happiness. Unfortunately, there was a perception that Sting was our family's secret, which was not true. Growing up without a diagnosis was more painful and complex than pretending we had a secret. My mother was courageous, and would have done anything to help her son. In fact, many years later, when I was confronted with the difficult decision to medicate my child, my mother's strength was immeasurable.

"Don't you think that if there had been a drug or anything that I could have given your brother so that he could have had a more normal life," she once told me, "that I would have given it to him?"

Sting's childhood had been stolen. He was stripped of his identity, continually beaten down without provocation. He found comfort and solace where he could, and one of those places was in comic books. My brother loved superheroes, especially the *Fantastic Four*. Never one to throw anything away, he read each comic book over and over until worn, threadbare pages hung loosely onto a single staple in the center of the book. We had an insider family joke where we'd tease Sting about being in love with Sue Richards, which he'd always deny, reminding us that she wasn't even real. Though he protested, he couldn't control the upward curl of the corner of his mouth, fighting hard to hide a giggle.

The world he knew was often cruel and frightening, and the *Fantastic Four* represented the family my brother always wanted. Superheroes could have protected him from the bullies back then—something his real family was unable to do.

CHAPTER 3

BRAIN TRAVELLING NEURONS ...DR. JOHN C. LILLY

The changes in our life must come from the
impossibility to live otherwise than according
to the demands of our conscience not from our
mental resolution to try a new form of life.
—LEO TOLSTOY

I n 1979, Sting discovered a new passion for bicycle riding. Actually, biking became an obsession he developed in part as a protest against the escalating gasoline prices. He could easily ride 100 miles a day and by late spring, he joined the League of American Wheelmen. The League was an organization that represented bicyclists, known as wheelmen in the 1800s, and created a movement to build safer roads, stronger communities, and a bicycle-friendly America. Sting spent every Sunday, weather permitting, riding all over Massachusetts with his pals from the League.

As for me, I continued trying to overcome my headache affliction and meditated for twenty minutes, twice daily. For several years, TM provided me with a break from the disproportionate amount of time I allocated to fear and pain, until the summer before my senior year in college, when the cluster headaches began to manifest with an immediate intensity. Feeling discouraged, my meditations became an inconsistent practice. *The black plains* seemed out of reach. Without warning or provocation, I'd suddenly feel a dagger stabbing me behind my eye or the torturous sensation of a clamp squeezing the back of my skull. The question of, *"What if I get another headache?"* became its own neurosis, almost as debilitating as an actual headache.

Western medicine hadn't served me well, but meditation, a centuries-old Eastern tradition, taught me that I had some control over my mind—which is why I was predisposed to mind-altering therapies. I was willing to try almost anything that could ameliorate my misery—including lysergic acid diethylamide (LSD).

Someone I had known from high school was interested in dating a friend of mine. I don't remember his name, but I became the messenger; the two of us shared all sorts of conversations with the intimacy that strangers often do. I have no recollection of how or even why we'd be talking about LSD, but we did, and he offered to get some acid for me—if I was interested. I said yes, and he sold me several tabs of blotter acid. I had no qualms or fears about taking acid, which, looking back now, seems kind of crazy. None of my friends did acid, nor did I ever discuss it with anyone other than my seller—who was just a guy I knew, not a friend. I was desperate to destroy the disabling pain that continued to thwart my happiness.

The first time I tried LSD was during the summer, on a Saturday. I remember because I had already planned to spend the day at Walden Pond with Bob Heller, one of my closest friends from high school. Spending time together during the first weekend home from college had become our tradition, and we'd either go to Walden or to Crane Beach.

By the time Bob picked me up at eleven thirty, the 6mm square piece of paper with a dot of LSD in the middle had dissolved on my tongue. Of course, as soon as I got into the car I told Bob that I had taken a hit of blotter acid.

At first, he just stared at me. "Really?" he asked, sort of half-smiling, trying to sublimate a sense of judgment or surprise. "Don't worry," he added, "I won't let anything bad happen to you." Bob knew me well; he knew that LSD wasn't outside the realm of something I might try. I wasn't particularly worried, but just in case, I was glad I was with him.

In less than thirty minutes, the LSD occupied my consciousness. *POW!* An unfamiliar burst of stimulation awakened my nervous system, with the sudden attention of a reveille bugle call. I began experiencing the rich intensity of colors, smells, and sounds for the first time. Acid amplified my thoughts, my senses, and erased my preoccupation with my physical being. I was whole, yet there was space between the abundance of activity in my brain and my body. Tripping put me in a state of acceptance and simply being—similar to how I felt in *the black plains*.

After walking around Walden Pond, Bob and I decided to drive up towards the North Shore to Crane Beach, in Ipswich, Massachusetts, less than an hour away. Bob was handsome, in a Rock Hudson sort of way, and he had been the captain of our high school swim team—I was in good hands going to the ocean with him.

Crane Beach and the Crane Estate boast more than five miles of trails of coastal dunes, and it is considered one of the finest and cleanest beaches on the East Coast. The water was always cold and clean—so clear that you could see the soft, white sand surround your feet like a pair of custom-fitted slippers. By the time we arrived at the beach, I was too caught up in my own thoughts to consider Bob's impression of me on LSD. I remember him smiling, sometimes giggling when he looked at me. For both Bob and me the most satisfying, wholesome experience at Crane's was pulling several of the golden, chestnut-colored, rubbery strips of kelp from the water and bringing them onto the beach. After several hours of sunbathing, we'd place the kelp on our face, and all over our body.

"Something so smooth, stretchy, and like gelatin has to be loaded with minerals from the ocean. I think we discovered a natural healing agent," Bob suggested. I agreed. The kelp had this cooling, almost healing effect on my skin, especially over my eyes. The seaweed was a gem from the ocean that someone at MIT would one day discover had huge untapped benefits.

The afternoon lingered with the seduction of the ocean salt infusing a crisp, insistent scent into the air. The water was cold, and the sun wrapped around us like layers of yellow chiffon. I didn't want the day to end. Being on acid, time had become somewhat irrelevant to me and I was content, swept up in this daydream.

Bob felt otherwise and explained, "It's already after five. I'm famished, and I need to eat."

I felt kind of speedy and extremely agreeable. "Okay, sure, let's get some food. I'm not too hungry, but I'm thirsty, and you're hungry, so let's go." We wiped the sand off our bodies and towels, grabbed our flip-flops, and threw away empty drink cans, leftover cheese, and crackers. After all, Crane's is a conservation site.

We drove back to Bob's house. There was so much traffic on Route 128 that it was almost 7:00 pm when we pulled into his driveway. He made himself a tuna sandwich; I ate a peach, some chips, and poured a glass of cold water from a pitcher in his fridge. It wasn't until we tried to play Scrabble that he became frustrated with me. In my present state of consciousness, I usurped an increasingly protracted amount of time during my turns. I had so much to consider—so many exciting variables with points and letters. *This word would open the board, this one might close it up*, I mused. I thrived on the intensity and concentrated on producing the most mind-boggling strategic word ever played in Scrabble. For Bob, the game became agonizingly slow, and by nine o'clock he offered to take me home.

I thanked Bob for an awesome day and walked into my house; back then, people in our neighborhood seldom locked their front door. I ran upstairs, said good night to my parents, showered, and changed into my pajamas; but I was still too stimulated to even think about sleep. I stayed up all night listening to music, writing, and doodling in my journal until morning. I discovered that, unfortunately, acid trips are time-consuming. It could take at least forty-eight hours before my mind and body could resume a hectic academic schedule. I couldn't depend on LSD if I wanted to finish senior year and graduate with honors. I'd need to find another way to get to that altered state of being; for now, TM and pain relievers would continue to be the inadequate therapy for my headaches.

During my senior year in college, I had taken a Medical Ethics class and read about neuroscientists and brain research studies from the 1950s and 1960s. I was particularly intrigued with Dr. John C. Lilly. His credentials were beyond reproach; his early brain research was conducted for the National Institute of Mental Health (NIMH) and other government agencies, including the U.S. Department of Defense. Lilly was more than a scientist, however; he was also a philosopher and a thought leader. His research confirmed that the human brain is malleable; we can change our brain and change our reality. I knew this was true because of my experience with *the black plains*, transcendental meditation, and LSD.

A year after I had graduated college, I remembered a quote I had read from Dr. Lilly, "The broader one's life experience, the easier it becomes to participate in life." Lisa Kay, a friend from Rutgers, convinced me that I'd have better luck finding a job in a big city; so in 1981, I moved from Boston to Los Angeles. She generously invited me to live with her until I found a job and could afford my own apartment. Several weeks after I moved in, Lisa went on location in Florida to work on a film and left me a note: *I'll be gone for six months. Feel free to use my car; keys on the counter.* I knew no one else in Los Angeles. This was my so-what-am-I-going-to-do-with-my-life post-college moment, and I had all the time that $2,500 dollars would allow to figure it out.

Having worked in the film industry since college, Lisa was fairly well connected, and often heard about temporary work opportunities through the grapevine. Her note gave me a number to call for a job, stating that the actress, Julie Newmar, who played the original Catwoman from the *Batman* television series, needed a temporary part-time assistant. Thanks to Lisa's tip I started working for Julie, but the temporary job ended two months later when I landed a full-time position as an assistant booking agent for college lecture tours. Finally, I was able to support myself and live on my own.

I felt secure in my new life and things were going well until I realized that the cluster headaches had moved with me to Los Angeles, and soon began keeping me awake at night. I couldn't let those headaches compromise my new job. Around this time, I had read an article in the *L.A. Weekly* about the Samadhi Floatation Center in Beverly Hills. A one-hour float in an isolation tank was supposed to be a natural and effective relaxation therapy, with benefits for those who suffered from chronic pain and lack of sleep. I signed up for six 60-minute sessions—based on the claims that the benefit of one float was equal to a full night of sleep. In Sanskrit, *Samadhi* means wholeness, the ultimate completion of consciousness.

At my first visit, the receptionist handed me a small plastic package containing a pair of earplugs. She led me down a narrow, semi-circular hallway to one of five private rooms, each one containing a shower cubicle and a small mirror hanging above a chair. The isolation tank on the floor resembled a hard plastic-coated storage box, rectangular in shape and accessible through a hatch-type door. The water inside the tank was 10" deep, maintained between ninety-three and ninety-four degrees Fahrenheit, and contained eight hundred pounds of dissolved Epsom salt. The density of this concentration provided buoyancy, making it easy to center your body in the tank and position your head so that your mouth and nose were above the water. The tank had its own filtration system, which circulated additional air from the room into the tank, leaving plenty of oxygen for normal breathing.

The float protocol involved first taking a shower before getting into the tank, then towel-drying my body. This process minimized body oil from contaminating the solution. I molded the disposable earplugs until the customized shape would seal my ears and prevent water from seeping in, thus avoiding a huge sensory distraction. My naked body slid into the chamber, gliding on top of the soothing water as Pachelbel's Cannon played through the tank's speakers. As the music synchronized in decrescendo, I took hold of the lock inside the door and slid the lever to the closed position until I was completely sealed in the warm luxury of borderless black. Eyes closed, my back, legs, and arms melted into a cradle of weightlessness.

It doesn't take long before your body tells your brain that something's about to happen and a sense of mild urgency races through your being. It reminded me of that precise moment of getting high, when your body tingles with excitement and a rush of something warm and seductive surges through your veins until the release, when brain and body slide together and apart in slow-motion mode. As that warmth filled my body in the tank, I understood this feeling of transcendence. In isolation and without distraction, my mind was unleashed and examined ideas with heightened intensity.

Sometimes I'd fall asleep in the tank until my limbs lightly twitched—making a small splash—in that jerking way limbs do when you're at the edge of slumber. The tank brought me deep into subconscious thought and I was able to focus on my inner perceptions. In these moments, I experienced the space between my physical and non-physical self, and similar to the way I had felt on LSD, I was still in control of my being. This invisible separation of consciousness and unconsciousness is a drug-like experience without taking drugs.

As Pachelbel's Cannon re-emerged, a soft glow of light appeared in the tank, marking the end of my session. Although each float following the first would be a slightly different experience, there was one constant: I would emerge as an observer after being in isolation. Once outside the building and back in bright daylight, it would take me six full minutes before I regained the coordination to walk to my car. I had to slowly ease my sensibilities into the saturation and stimulation of my surroundings.

Going to the tanks became a weekly morning habit. Floating made me feel better and helped me cope with the headaches, and each session reminded me that I had some control over my brain. As a frequent floater, the receptionist would occasionally break the privacy rules and tell me if celebrities were there. Once, my float appointment was scheduled at the same time as Jack Nicholson's. I attempted to send him my brain waves, telepathy in a tank. *Hi, Jack, it's me. I'm floating in the tank in Room #2.* I waited patiently, but no telepathic messages came back. *Nothing. Nada from Jack.*

It wasn't long before I was promoted to a booking agent. I was told that my first client, a neuroscientist, had developed a way for humans to communicate with dolphins. This was well beyond a crazy coincidence. Dr. John C. Lilly, who invented the sensory deprivation tank in 1954, would become, in late 1981, my first client. I would soon learn about

Dr. Lilly's significant contributions to neuroscience and the wide-reaching importance of his work with dolphins.

Lilly had become a highly regarded scientist in the 1940s and 1950s, having invented an electrical capacitance manometer, a device for measuring blood pressure, and gas concentration and flow meters to study respiration, pressure, and altitude for the US Navy during World War II. He later became interested in neuroscience and studied the physical structures of the brain and consciousness. In 1951, he published a paper detailing a way to display patterns of brain electrical activity on a cathode ray display screen, using extremely thin electrodes, which he devised for insertion into a living brain. His research on the electrical stimulation of the nervous system introduced biphasic balanced pulses, now known as Lilly's waveforms. Using biphasic pulses is currently the established approach for safe electrical stimulation in neuroprosthetics, and is the best way to avoid tissue damage and metal electrode electrolysis. Lilly's prodigious research included electronic brain stimulation, studying dreams, schizophrenia, and the neurophysiology of motivation.

During his training in psychoanalysis at NIMH, Lilly embarked upon experiments involving sensory deprivation. There had been an open question in neurophysiology as to what keeps the brain going and the origin of its energy sources, more simply known as consciousness. One hypothesis was that the energy sources were biological and internal, independent of the outside environment, and that if all stimuli were cut off, the brain would simply go to sleep. Lilly challenged this theory and created an environment, the sensory deprivation tank, which isolated an individual from all external stimulation. Deprived of external stimuli, Lilly concluded, the brain does, in fact, generate its own experiences.

Throughout the 1950s and 1960s, there was an explosion of research being conducted on the brain. Chemist Alfred Hoffman worked for the Swiss pharmaceutical company Sandoz, researching respiration; this led to him isolating and synthesizing ergotamine compounds with other organic molecules. The 25th lysergic acid combination became known as LSD-25; the purest and most potent formulation of the drug. LSD was marketed to neuroscientists and psychologists as a way to investigate the workings of the brain and the experience of psychosis.

Lilly continued his neuro-chemical research, immersing himself in the floatation tank in his laboratory for extended periods while under the influence of LSD. He believed that a scientist should never conduct an experiment or procedure on another person that they had not first conducted on themselves. His goal was to experience the soul in alternate realities, so he used LSD to chemically reconfigure his neurons in order to disrupt the connection between the brain and body, in order to connect with the "soul essence," or inner-consciousness. The results led to his premise that our survival as a species depended on our evolution, which required inter-species communication. His research identified dolphins as the mammals most suitable and similar to us in terms of our central nervous system. He excluded whales, believing that they'd be unwieldy to work with as subjects. Based on his algorithm of brain size to body mass, dolphins were the most intelligent mammals. A dolphin's cerebral cortex—which encompasses about two-thirds of brain mass and controls hearing, touch, vision, and cognitive functions like thinking, perceiving, and understanding language—is forty percent larger than a human's.

During May 8–10, 1965, at The Second International Conference on the Use of LSD in Psychotherapy and Alcoholism, hosted by the South Oaks Research Foundation in Amityville, New York, Dr. Lilly delivered one of his highly regarded published studies. Dr. Freemont-Smith, founder of the Macy Foundation led these conferences. Thought leaders in psychotherapy attended from around the world to share diverse perspectives on medical research without government intervention.

Lilly presented his paper, a case study about a dolphin called Elvar. Dolphins are a very social species, but Elvar was not functioning on any level. Lilly went into the pool with this massive mammal and met Elvar in his element, and got very close to him in a physical sense. According to the transcripts from the conference, Lilly explained, "The important thing for us with the LSD in the dolphin is that meaning (communication) resides completely in this non-verbal exchange." Lilly employed a woman who lived in the tank with Elvar 24 hours a day, for a week. The tank had enough water for Elvar to swim and was shallow enough for the woman to stand. Using LSD to unleash Elvar's inhibition and a supporting, maternal, loving type of therapy resulted in great success. It wasn't long before Elvar joyfully preferred swimming with humans, and reconnected with his fellow *Tursiops*.

After Lilly's presentation, Freemont-Smith agreed, "This seems to me to fit so closely with what we have been learning about the needs of human beings who are being treated with LSD. I am delighted with it."

Another conference participant was Miss Mary Wicks, a probation officer/social worker from Worcester, England. She was fascinated by Lilly's talk about dolphins because, as she stated, "It is so close to my own experiences working with delinquents and people who have been so damaged that they can't trust or relate to anybody. I know from experience in working with these people for years, who never give in, and who always hit back at society, and I have had the same experience you had. After one or two treatments with LSD they are feeling for the first time that they are actually relating, and that it is possible to get near someone, and that it is all part of the process of loving and then being able to accept love."

Although I was the junior booking agent, I was expected to spend face time with a client before a tour. I began watching early film footage of Lilly with the dolphins, read several of his early books, papers from scientific conferences, and published articles from various journals. One of the reasons why Lilly was a popular request for the college lecture circuit was the recent theatrical release of the sci-fi movie *Altered States*, which was based on his book about the research he conducted in isolation tanks under the influence of hallucinogens like ketamine (Vitamin K) and LSD. The film featured the acting debut of both William Hurt and Drew Barrymore, and critics considered the theatrical release filled with an aggressive audio mix and visual pyrotechnics more of a horror sci-fi flick than a serious Hollywood film. Nonetheless, the film generated enough press for me to book a dozen dates for a college lecture tour.

I was both excited and intimidated to meet my own psychedelic Dr. Doolittle in person. Lilly was smart—crazy smart—and arguably one of the pioneers who understood consciousness and how to change one's brain in a way that would result in connection, rather than isolation from humanity. Lilly once wrote, "You don't have to suffer continual chaos in order to grow." It had become my greatest challenge to at least contain the suffering and chaos in my life.

Of course, I was a Lilly groupie—after all, HE invented the tank that brought me to *the black plains* that provided me with peace and relief from pain. Yes, I had a job to do, and yes, the dolphins were cool. But Dr. John Lilly was the only person I knew who had the credentials to validate my personal bias, which included psychedelic drug use and alternative therapies that expanded my sense of self and provided me with a respite from my distress.

Driving on Highway 1 alongside the ocean to Lilly's home in Pacific Palisades, with the sun animating the sparkling, light-blue color of the sky, led me onto a canyon road. I think I had driven 1,000 feet above sea level; my ears popped, and Lisa's Volkswagen Beetle seemed unsure, due to the great acceleration already expended to reach our current elevation. The car had a stick shift and I was concerned that it didn't have the power to make it up the last incline. There was nothing but overgrown canyon brush between my location and my destination. Finally, I made it to the only house on the top of the hill. I wondered why anyone would choose to live so high on this isolated road before concluding that it was probably so they could be closer to God.

Lilly's wife and business partner, Toni, greeted me warmly at the door and gestured for me to come inside. Her eyes reflected her unpretentious demeanor, and her golden-tan complexion accentuated her natural beauty. She reminded me of those 60-year-old women whose elegance is enhanced by their age.

"John was just out with the dolphins," she said with an engaging smile. "He's cleaning up, but he'll be down in a minute."

I followed her into the kitchen, where she busied herself making fresh lemonade. The front façade of the sprawling ranch had a spectacular vista of the Pacific Ocean. Moments later, Lilly walked in and Toni introduced us. He was rather good-looking, with bronze skin, blue eyes behind wire-rimmed glasses, and tousled, gray hair. He looked fit in his t-shirt, shorts, and sandals.

"Trouble finding the house?" he asked. "Everyone does."

Before I could even respond, he and Toni engaged in private dialogue describing previous misadventures with famous friends like actor Burgess Meredith, who would get hopelessly lost trying to navigate Toni's directions.

"Well, she's here," Toni proudly stated.

"We can talk outside," Lilly mumbled. I had to listen carefully to understand him.

We walked along a short grassy path in front of the house that overlooked the ocean. Two folding plastic chairs were set up near his isolation tank, which looked more like an army relic than the light-colored, lightweight tank I floated in at the Center. It appeared especially tall, as though one might need a step stool to climb inside.

"Toni mentioned you were just out with the dolphins," I began. "Sorry to have interrupted your work on such a beautiful day." He remained quiet as I showed him artwork that I unrolled from the cardboard tube I had on my lap. "We need your approval on the posters and brochures for the tour," I said, reminding him of the reason for my visit.

His eyes carefully examined the artwork on the poster, and without looking at me, he began speaking in what interviewers from previous articles I had read about him referred to as "John speak":

> "*Sorry* is a word humans use but it only takes up space," he said. "What are you *sorry* for? After all, I agreed to meet with you." He looked at me, drank some of his lemonade, and handed the approved poster back to me. "We humans have trouble knowing what to say, and when we speak, we don't say what we mean."

I felt uncomfortable, intimidated. It's difficult to have a conversation with a neuroscience rock star.

Lilly's college lecture presentation included amazing black-and-white film footage of his early work with dolphins. He used sonic video inputs and outputs both underwater and on land, a keyboard, and a minicomputer interfaced with the two species. His team's work revealed digitized dolphin-human speech similarities, which resulted in the successful completion of a forty whistle-word vocabulary shared between humans and dolphins.

Finishing his lemonade, John then mused about the possibility that since dolphins have been around for millions of years, they've likely spent much of their time meditating. "What else would they be doing?" he proposed with a chuckle.

I wondered, *Does each dolphin have his or her own mantra?*

I began to feel a bit more comfortable with Lilly, and just as I was about to share with him my history of floating, Toni came outside to tell him that he had received the phone call he was expecting; this was also my cue to leave. I was actually grateful for the interruption because it would have been inappropriate and groupie-like of me to babble on about my personal experiences in the float tank.

Driving back to the office, the thing that struck me most about Lilly was his intensity and vitality. His calendar included meetings with people he referred to as "physicist friends at various universities who keep me informed"; presentations for his Human Dolphin Foundation, and occasional lectures at the Esalen Institute in Big Sur, California. During his career, Lilly formed close bonds with Nobel Prize-winning physicists Richard Feynman and Robert Milliken, philosopher Buckminster Fuller, and psychotherapy pioneers R. D. Laing and Fritz Perls. Although he traveled a great deal, he committed to a list of available dates, which we managed to book.

Like dolphins, I am certain that humans possess an inner sanctum deep within the many layers nestled inside our brain. We exist somewhere in the space between our conscious and our unconscious selves. Some of us may never consciously connect with this deep soul level, while others are frightened by it. I'm in the group of those who spend their lives trying to understand it. Throughout my adolescence, my headaches imprisoned me in a solitary confinement; but the other side of that torment led me to find my inner sanctum.

The various treatments that were available to me at that time—like psychoactive drugs; psychedelic drugs; drugs for prophylaxis, like ergotamine sublingual tablets; transcendental meditation; and floating in isolation—all provided me with ways to alter the neural pathways in my brain so that I could see things differently and change my reality. I know for a fact that we can exert some control over our minds and our bodies. How am I so certain? Because I have done it: I haven't had a cluster headache since 1993.

CHAPTER 4

THAT OLD MAGIC TRICK
...DR. DACHER KELTNER

The most authentic thing about us is our capacity
to create, to overcome, to endure, to transform,
to love and be greater than our suffering.
—BEN OKRI

S ometimes a situation appears and we just fall into it as though it were simply waiting for us. Like an automatic door, the opportunity opens by our presence, the result of momentum from previous choices we've made and from lessons learned in younger moments. We evolve into who we are through our actions, and it is our humanity and our sense of purpose that connect us to the next big moment. One of my next big moments came in 1983 when I began working for the rock band Aerosmith, and I learned something new about the brain. I witnessed the ravages of drug addiction and the life-altering power of resilience.

In 1984, the band was trying to stage a reunion and a comeback since disbanding in 1979; a time punctuated with missed interviews, demolished hotel rooms, and truncated or cancelled concert dates. Wild forces both united and divided the "Bad Boys from Boston," a talented group of artists revered for their classic blues-influenced brand of rock and roll. Tim Collins, the band's new manager, had been trying to harness those forces for a tour: the BACK IN THE SADDLE tour.

Without a record deal, the band embarked on a highly successful string of dates, twenty-four sold-out shows in cities across the country, which provided the band an opportunity to showcase its live talent. I was hired to oversee tour publicity and promotion, which wasn't easy because Aerosmith was better remembered by the press for its problems than its music. One of those problems was Joe Perry's heroin-induced seizure when his solo band, The Joe Perry Project, played the Chateau Madrid in North Carolina. During the well-documented night in 1982, Joe, while performing onstage with the white spotlight beaming on him, suddenly went stiff as a board, fell to the floor, and was thought to be dead. Tim flew Joe to the Lodge in Westwood, Massachusetts, that night, for rehabilitation.

Joe had been candid about his past, and I was awed by his resilience. Just two years earlier, Joe had lost practically everything: his previous wife, his previous manager, and his previous record deal. He could barely stand on stage while fronting The Joe Perry Project, and he had very little income beyond what Tim supplemented. I never knew that Joe Perry. The person I met in late 1983 was getting his life back together.

The success of the BACK IN THE SADDLE dates attracted the attention of Geffen Records, and in 1985, the original members of Aerosmith released its first album in six years, *Done With Mirrors*. The band included Steven Tyler, Joe Perry, Tom Hamilton, Brad Whitford, and Joey Kramer. Just before the release of *Done With Mirrors* in March 1985, Joe, Tom, and I flew to Toronto to meet with Stan Kulin, the president of Warner-Elektra-Atlantic (WEA) Canada, and the band's international record distributor. The overnight promotion tour was efficient and left no down time in the schedule; there would be no late-night clubbing or getting into drugs on my watch! We arrived at the Four Seasons Hotel by 10:30 p.m., and the following day began with an 8:00 a.m. wake-up call for a 9:00 a.m. stop at the WEA office.

Stan was a well-respected and well-known corporate executive in the music industry. As he greeted us in the WEA lobby, he stood over six feet tall and he exuded a larger-than-life presence.

"Hi, Joe," he began as he introduced himself. "I bet you don't remember what happened the last time we met."

"Help me out a little," Joe said. "When was that?" Joe was warm, with a quick, dry wit attached to his Boston accent that further embellished his personality when he spoke.

"We met the last time you were up here in 1979, just before *Draw the Line*."

"Uh oh, here it comes," Joe said, with an all too familiar response, another reminder about his less than flattering past. "I can't say that I remembah very much from those days, but I'm guessin' it wasn't very good."

"Let me remind you," Stan insisted. "You were drunk. Very drunk. You tripped and slammed into me, and the drink in your hand ended up on my pants. I was holding you up, as you were standing on my shoe with the heel of your boot."

Joe shook Stan's hand, looked him in the eyes and said, "Hey, man, at least I was standin'—which was unusual back then."

After a momentary pause, Stan, the rest of the WEA group, and Tom began laughing. I wasn't sure where this would go, and held my breath before I awkwardly smiled. *Good grief, Joe,* I thought. *This is how the man who'll be selling your new album in Canada remembers you?*

To his benefit, Joe's response was priceless. He acknowledged that Stan had likely recounted the event accurately, and then apologized.

"I'm truly sorry, man. I hope I didn't cause you too much pain. Hey, now I can pay for your dry cleanin.'"

Stan swung his arm around Joe as if they were old buddies. Just like that, the new and improved Aerosmith was on its way to being welcomed, rather than avoided. I couldn't believe how Joe had turned his life around. He looked healthy, happy, and seemed grateful for this second chance.

Overall, I thought things were going well and I enjoyed working for the band. Steven and Joe, both incredibly bright, had a hilarious shtick together. We shared lots of laughter over Steven's impromptu limericks that often went on and on and on. Steven knew how to push Joe's buttons and several times, when they were live on camera, Joe would be cracking up as Steven continued his rhyming banter. For example, one Christmas I had given the band members red felt bags filled with candy that looked like chunks of coal. Of course this was meant to be a joke. Steven responded with the perfect thank you note.

> We loved your little buckets of coal
> although it was tasty, Twas Very droll
> You're so good at your job
> Just like cracking a safe
> Well just leave this alone
> Owe it all to ~~Good~~ Blind Faithe (inside joke)

What I didn't realize then was how profoundly trouble seemed to plague them, like a contagious virus. They were all contaminated, but Steven's illness was the most deeply rooted.

During the last month of the worldwide DONE WITH MIRRORS tour, some dates were cancelled, and in late spring of 1986, the band returned home to Boston. Unfortunately, the past stuck to their heels like black, sticky tar. Too much drinking and heroin, in-fighting, and sloppy performances gave rise to serious concerns about the band's stability. Worst of all was the fact that Steven was seen hitting the methadone clinic every day at 7:00 a.m., just as it opened. Methadone is a synthetic analgesic, a long-acting drug, similar to morphine, and used as a substitute drug to help patients wean off heroin. By late afternoon, Steven would snap out of his methadone stupor but would often miss scheduled band meetings. The other band members were fed up with this routine and talked about replacing Steven on the next album. Aerosmith was like your favorite childhood teddy bear: limply held together with clumps of threaded knots from the many surgeries performed to replace the stuffing.

Tim saw the band spinning wildly out of control and knew what had to be done. Each of the band members would have to get healthy, but helping Steven was the most immediate concern. Tim met with a New York psychologist experienced in the process of intervention, a technique designed to assist a family or business group to effectively deal with the destructive power of addictive disorders. As soon as he returned from New York, Tim scheduled an offsite meeting with Joe, Tom, Brad, and Joey.

He explained that Steven was sick; his addiction a mental illness and it needed treatment. Tim's intensity was infectious. By distinguishing the difference between Steven and the illness, he was able to enlist the support of the other band members, and the wheels for an intervention were set in motion. Tim made the band a promise: if they all got clean, Aerosmith would be the biggest rock band in the world by 1990. The second part of this pre-intervention meeting involved several staff members, myself included. Tim explained the plan and process for what would be Steven's intervention.

Each band member was instructed to write down specific examples of how and when Steven's addiction affected him. The main concern was that the psychologist Tim hired couldn't mediate an intervention if Steven was high, but unfortunately, in those days, he was almost always high. Tim had to ensure that even if Steven were jonesing for a fix, he'd be in the office—without his morning shot of methadone.

With a sense of urgency, Tim asked me to book European media—something significant enough to get Steven into the office by six EST the next morning. The BBC had previously extended an open invitation to interview Steven and Joe, and due to the time difference, a live interview with the British network was the most compelling way, without arousing suspicion, to get Steven in the office before the methadone clinic opened. Tim confirmed with Steven that he and Joe would be in the office for the live interview at 6:00 a.m. Everything was at stake: Steven's life, other band members' addiction issues, their careers and income, their wives, families, and dozens of others—including me—who depended on Aerosmith for their livelihood. I made the call, but I dreaded going into the office the next morning.

Steven stumbled in at 6:00 a.m. wearing sunglasses and looking disheveled from being up all night. Totally dumbfounded, he walked into the conference room, wondering aloud why the rest of the band was sitting around the conference room table with yellow legal pads in front of them as if they were preparing for something to happen. Everyone knew about the plan except for Steven and his girlfriend. A bag had been packed with all of Steven's essentials, and a chartered plane was waiting to take him that day to a rehabilitation facility in rural Pennsylvania's Amish country, where a bed had already been assigned to him. Whatever each band member wrote on their pads of paper would ultimately need to matter enough to Steven to make him go to rehab within the next several hours.

Tim had previously explained to the staff that the length of the intervention was unpredictable, but somehow Sandy, Tim's assistant, and I got it in our heads that they might be finished by 1:00 p.m. During that time, we sat wondering what they could possibly be discussing and arguing about for hours. During a break at eleven thirty, Tim called me into the conference room. Out of habit, I imagine, he wanted to check in with me and hear what was going on, even though he already knew the answer: *nothing*. This intervention was sealed as tightly as a ziplock bag, and I hadn't heard about any media rumors or leaks. There hadn't been any calls from the record label.

I walked into this room like I was observing a scene in cinema verité. The room felt hollow, like they were all in a black hole disconnected from the universe. Something separated me from them; I was glad to be invisible in there. I glanced at Tom, the band's bass guitarist who was nicknamed "the professor" because he was always reading books, magazines, and newspapers in limos on the way to an interview, or while waiting for a band meeting to begin. Tom was thoughtful and exuded somewhat of a calming influence, but today he seemed lost, overwhelmed. He wasn't one for drama, and I imagined an animated word bubble hanging over his head: *"Man, who knows how this thing will end up?"*

Joey and Brad had their backs to me, and I stopped short as my eyes locked on Joe. Dressed in his typical black shirt, black leather jacket, and black skinny jeans, his attire had its usual ready-to-rock look. As Steven would say, "Joe just rolls out of bed and looks cool." But that day, he didn't. Joe's face revealed only misery, gut-wrenching rot. Known in the press as the "toxic twins," Steven and Joe were, at times, as close as brothers, two souls inextricably bound together through heaven and hell. Steven was sitting, his frame eclipsed by the humongous size of the executive chair.

He seemed intent on something he was writing, and didn't acknowledge me at all. I couldn't wait to get out of that room oozing with anger, fear, and pain, with so much riding on the outcome of decisions and words yet to be said. My heart ached for Steven—for all of them.

I crouched beside Tim's chair. "Are you okay?" I whispered.

He responded with a slight nod. "Yes. It's gonna be a while."

He was more tentative than I expected. Tim had a way of making things right, but this was out of his hands. Steven wasn't going easily, and everyone's fate rested on his mercurial moods. Tim asked me to wait in my office until they were further along. Some sort of official announcement would be required—and I would be the one to send it—but it was still too soon for me to tell how this day would end.

By now, Tim's phones were ringing off the hook and Sandy maintained as much order as possible while fielding calls from the band members' wives. I returned to my office, where I gazed at memorabilia from better times with Aerosmith, including a 1985 autographed photo with "Marvelous" Marvin Hagler, the undisputed World Middleweight Boxing Champion since 1980, in the ring at the Boston Garden. I had negotiated a promotion for "My Fist Your Face," a song from the *Done With Mirrors* album, which became Marvelous Marvin's theme song, played before every boxing match at The Garden. His note on the photograph read, *I always have faith.* Both Aerosmith and Hagler were local heroes at that time, and soon "My Fist Your Face" became anthemic, playing during Boston Celtics basketball and Boston Bruins hockey games.

How far they had fallen since then. I couldn't believe that they had been given this once-in-a-lifetime second chance—and they blew it again! There is nothing dignified about being a junkie. It can be so easy to become blinded by insanity and lose sight of one's humanity. Before long, every waking thought is consumed with the quest for the next hit. You must stay high, you believe, because the terror of being thrown off that precipice is like falling into an inferno. Interventions lead you to confronting your unmet despair, the agony imprisoned in your heart for years, burning like a secret. You're not even sure what it is because you've never spoken about it to anyone—not your brother, not your priest, not your lover.

According to Sartre, "Human life begins on the far side of despair." After nearly ten long, excruciating hours, Steven agreed to begin anew and go to rehab. The intervention was successful and by 5:00 p.m. he was on his way to spending forty-five days at the facility in Pennsylvania.

The Steven Tyler I knew was wicked smart, hilarious, and ridiculously talented. As early as the BACK IN THE SADDLE tour, I was surprised by the band's personal involvement in select charitable organizations and their work with veterans and people with disabilities. One of my priorities for every concert, per the band's instruction, was to ensure that anyone with a disability or anyone who had served our country and had purchased tickets to the show would receive the best seats in the house. Closer to show time, Steven would always double check to make sure we took care of those kinds of important accommodations. Like a crack of light seen escaping from a door, altruism and compassion seeped from Steven's soul. I hoped that those qualities would give him strength while he was in Pennsylvania.

My feelings about the intervention, at that time, were mixed. It was a necessary tough love plan to keep Steven alive—if not to wholly bring him back to a rewarding life and a successful career. However, each of the band members needed to get clean, and I could only imagine Steven seeing the hypocrisy of the intervention being about him. Although I've always had conflicting feelings about how this manifested, Aerosmith was lucky to have, in Tim, someone who was in this for the long journey ahead.

Shortly after Steven was in rehab, the rest of the band members went into addiction programs. While the band was in rehab, I had no work, and in 1987, Tim and I parted ways. When I first began working for Aerosmith, I was twenty-four years old. Tim affectionately used to call me "Young Faithe." At the time, I was too naïve to comprehend the scope of what was happening to the band members and how much their lives would change. They had endured decades of being chased by shadows of betrayal and darkness, but I had been shielded from much of the lunacy. I was only there to see the effects of its devastating aftermath.

Nonetheless, I didn't expect my job with Aerosmith to end with the entire band going into rehab. Working for a band on tour is more personal, emotional, and intimate than a typical job that you leave at the end of the day. I felt abandoned by a community in which I no longer had a place. I harbored this alienation and stomped my Aerosmith experience into a crevasse in the pavement of my career. I moved on with my life. However, it wasn't until I attended a lecture in Santa Monica at The Center for Effective Learning (C4EL) by Dr. Dacher Keltner, a University of California, Berkeley, psychology professor, when I realized that having participated in Steven's intervention provided me with an important life lesson about resilience.

Keltner is renowned for his research studying human emotion, the neuroscience of happiness, and what it means to be human. In 2001, he co-founded The Greater Good Science Center (GGSC) at Berkeley, and launched its newsletter and website, "To promote the study and development of human happiness, compassion, and prosocial behavior through the dissemination of scientific, educational, and parenting resources." The website provides an array of award-winning media including articles, videos, books, podcasts, newsletters, surveys, and interactive quizzes. The California state-funded wing of the early mental health initiative, Time for Kids, uses the GGSC website to help teach and counsel children in over 400 schools. The GGSC also serves as a bridge between social scientists and parents, educators, community leaders, and policy makers. I participated in a free Greater Good Science Center online class, hosted by Keltner and Dr. Emiliana Simon-Thomas. The course featured presentations by luminaries like Paul Ekman, Jon Kabat-Zinn, and Barbara Fredrickson. The Center also sponsors daylong events, such as one that featured Dr. Shauna Shapiro and Dr. Dan Siegel: Mindfulness, Connection, and Compassion; and during the 2015 holiday season the GGSC launched an NPR radio special, *The Science of Gratitude*, narrated by Susan Sarandon. This is the mecca of the neuroscience of good, and what it means to be human.

Keltner's research reveals that over time, we humans evolved into social beings, a nomenclature that shares an innate power of human emotion, and connects us to one another through altruism—this selfless concern for the well-being of others. His research, and that of other scientists, suggest that the activation of the vagus nerve, a bundle of nerves that originates in the top of the spinal cord, is associated with feelings of caretaking and the ethical intuition that humans from different social groups (even adversarial ones) share a common humanity. He further explains how managing our emotions, forging forgiveness, and building resilience can contribute to a happier, more meaningful life, and we receive significant emotional rewards when acting for the benefit of others, even when it means operating against our own self-interest. Reflecting on this became a moment, a memory cut with precision. Although I no longer worked for Aerosmith, and suffered as a result of their choices, I wanted them all to be well; I wanted them all to succeed.

The neurobiology behind the activation of the vagus nerve produces "...that feeling of warm expansion in the chest—for example, when we are moved by someone's goodness or when we appreciate a beautiful piece of music," Keltner explained to the small group of parents and teachers in Santa Monica at the C4EL.

"The vagus nerve," he continued, "is thought to stimulate certain muscles in the vocal chamber, enabling communication. Very new science suggests that it may be closely connected to receptor networks for oxytocin, a neurotransmitter involved in trust and maternal bonding."

Listening to beautiful music, being around those who are morally inspiring, or walking through a meadow or a trail in the woods all enhance our sense of purpose. A purposeful existence connects us to one another and our shared humanity.

According to Keltner, "Awe is the ultimate 'collective' emotion, for it motivates people to do things that enhance the greater good." I think this is part of the reason why we revere rock stars. In a huge concert arena we are connected to 30,000 other like-minded people. We're vested in each other for several hours, uplifted by this larger experience, inspired by this greater shared musical experience—and it's awesome!

True to his word, Tim kept his promise to the band. Steven, Joe, Tom, Brad, and Joey got clean and by 1990, Aerosmith was arguably the biggest rock band in the world. A wife and mother by then, and a senior executive at Bertelsmann, a multinational media company, I watched with what I can only describe as awe.

Over the years, I've maintained intermittent contact with Tim and several members of Aerosmith. When my son was born in 1996, Tim and the band sent me an unforgettable gift; a package filled with customized baby onesies with the Aerosmith logo across the front, and other one-of-a-kind items. I am happy and grateful that our collective lives became more enriched than we probably thought possible.

These days, when I hear certain Aerosmith songs on the radio or when I see Steven being a judge on *American Idol*, it activates my vagus nerve. I remember one *American Idol* show in particular when James Durbin, the rock singer with Tourette's and Asperger's brilliantly covered Aerosmith's quintessential ballad "Dream On." Steven was visibly blown away by Durbin's vocal performance, just as I and the rest of America were that night. It may seem puerile that watching a singing competition on television could evoke in me feelings of connection and happiness, but it did. For the first time, I appreciated what Steven had been through, and I could see how his resilience had enabled him to reinvent himself and experience more love, altruism, and fulfillment in his sixties than he had perhaps experienced during his entire four-decades-long career.

In ways I couldn't have imagined, Aerosmith taught me what it means to be resilient. Twice the band made millions and soared beyond rock stardom, only to lose everything. For a time, the only VACANCY sign for Aerosmith was at a rehab facility, a place where they would endure loneliness until their physical and emotional suffering slowly set them free. I imagine they cheated the Grim Reaper on several occasions, yet each time they re-emerged and reconnected as Aerosmith, the bond of their collective resilience became stronger. Each one of the nearly fifty times I heard Steven sing "Dream On" live, it was like I was hearing it for the first time. The prophetic lyric, *"Dream on, dream on, dream on, dream until your dream comes true,"* helped bolster the resilience I would need to rely on in the future.

Recently, a friend asked me, "How have you survived? How have you gotten your family through the pandemonium of mental health crises?" I reflected back on what I learned from Aerosmith during the *DONE WITH MIRRORS* tour, the long-awaited reunion that moved so many people. I didn't respond to my friend's question, but I thought about what I might have said. *"It's like that old magician's trick, an illusion, done with smoke and mirrors."* Working for Aerosmith, I had developed resilience; I kept moving forward, holding onto the hope that we would find our way out of the labyrinth of mental illness.

CHAPTER 5

MR. TOAD'S WILD RIDE...
DR. TIMOTHY LEARY

*We must be willing to let go of the life we have
planned, so as to have the life that is waiting for us.*
—E. M. FORSTER

There was a time after I left Aerosmith when I thought that I had also left mental health issues far behind. My brother's *normal* included working, bike riding, and making weekly plans with his age-appropriate MENSA friends. My life, too, was fulfilling. My headaches were more of a memory than a reality, and I enjoyed a meaningful career in the music business working at The David Geffen Company, then tenure with Rhino Entertainment. I reconnected with Steven, a man I had met in Los Angeles many years earlier. We fell in love, and we got married in 1990. Three years later, on New Year's Eve in 1993, our wonderful son Ben was born. Two years later, our beautiful son Cooper completed our family.

In those early days, the four of us spent every weekend together going on adventures to the park, the tar pits, or the beach in Malibu to visit relatives. My boys loved the outdoors, and together, we made enduring memories such as hiking for pollywogs, bringing them home in glass jars, and nurturing them in a homemade terrarium until they turned into frogs. Eventually we'd find dead, petrified frog remains under the fridge or the dryer. Life seemed wholly normal, and there were no signs of the tsunami that was about to come our way.

Ben had always been shy, and much more anxious and reserved than other 9-year-old boys. Yet his outside demeanor reflected calm and he was easy to be around, charming everyone with his consistently happy disposition. Yes, things were delightful—until one unforgettable Saturday afternoon. Ben and Cooper were playfully running around the house, then suddenly, like a pinprick popping a balloon, the carefree sounds of laughter became shrieks of terror, screams for help.

I ran downstairs to the boys' bedroom. Ben's big, green eyes were inflated, the pallor of his face changing from tones of beige to red. He clenched his neck, pulling at the skin near his Adam's apple as huge teardrops flowed from his eyes.

"Help me, Mummy, please help me!" he cried. "I can't breathe!" He continued pinching the skin at his throat, but the rest of his body was immobile. "I need to go to the hospital! My heart hurts, and I'm so scared!" He grabbed my arms tightly, like a blood pressure cuff. My heart began palpitating. I tried my best to conceal my fear; but as I examined Ben I saw no bleeding, no cuts, and no broken bones. Still, I was terrified.

Ben's pediatrician referred us to a psychiatrist. He explained that Ben's horrifying episode was a panic attack. According to the NIMH, *"Panic attacks are characterized by a fear of disaster or of losing control even when there is no danger present. They can occur any time and sufferers worry about and dread the next onslaught."* Ben was prescribed

Prozac to manage his anxiety. However, after two days on the drug, I suddenly heard the crashing sound of terra cotta pots being smashed on our kitchen tile floor. My sweet, gentle son was freaking out on the Prozac. I called the psychiatrist, who prescribed a different anti-anxiety, anti-depressant, called Celexa. He casually mentioned another young patient of his, also on Prozac, "who ran right through his parents' glass door," and that was the last time we saw that shrink. The one thing I realized that afternoon was how little I knew about Ben's anxiety. We had no idea what a panic attack was, or if it might happen again.

After four months on Celexa, and no more panic attacks or "feeling plastic," Ben's anxiety had greatly diminished and calm had returned to our lives. We settled back into a routine, and the boys enjoyed a great summer going to day camp and having sleepovers with their friends. We had moved past Ben's panic attacks, which were so frightening at the time that it was impossible for us to imagine how much more punishing mental illness could be—then unexpectedly, Cooper's brain changed. He began to make strange noises that sounded like a dog's bark or a mouse's squeak. At first, it seemed as though he was trying to clear his throat, and these noises might possibly be a reaction to the hot, arid summer weather. However, these vocalizations were the precursor to what would become prominent vocal tics.

Over the next ten months, Cooper saw several different psychiatrists and psychologists. The questions I would ask about each new prescription became almost rhetorical, because there were never any answers:

What does anyone know about the long-term impact of this drug or its side effects? After ten months, why aren't Cooper's tics getting better? Some of his meds caused significant weight gain and some caused significant weight loss. Isn't this harmful to a developing body?

Finally, one of our neighbors, and now our close friend, Carol, told us we were wasting our time. "You need to take him to a neurologist for those tics," she said, and she was right. Cooper needed a proper diagnosis so that we could better understand the reason behind his random movements and erratic behavior. He needed appropriate treatment.

Cooper was seven years old when he went to UCLA's Resnick Neuropsychiatric Institute (NPI) for a 2-day evaluation with highly respected neuropsychiatric research scientist Dr. James McCracken, Director of the Division of Child and Adolescent Psychiatry Resnick NPI. During those two consecutive afternoons, Cooper spent some of his time behind one-way observation windows. His tics were slightly less pronounced than they had been earlier in the week; his eyes twitched, his arm and neck jerked, and he kept clearing his throat. McCracken didn't diagnose Cooper; instead, he recommended a therapist for his "anger issues." I was shocked, livid that this highly regarded and deeply experienced specialist couldn't see that Cooper had Tourette's syndrome.

It would be an additional three months before Cooper would be diagnosed with Tourette's, when the presentation and duration of his motor and/or vocal tics exhibited *uninterrupted* for at least a year. This was the diagnostic criterion in the *DSM-4*, published in 1994.

No one, not the psychiatrists nor the specialists, had any answers, and our lives became a dangerous drug experiment. I didn't want my son to be on these trial-and-error drugs; no one really understood how these pills interacted with all the chemical compounds in the brain. At that time, there were only a handful of neurologists in the country with extensive experience in treating children with complex Tourette's symptoms and prescribing medication cocktails.

Cooper was nine years old when we met Dr. Erik, whose office was in the UCLA Medical Center. After waiting a month for a two-session medical history appointment, Dr. Erik was the charter member of our

"A" team. His obvious intelligence and sensitivity about the impact of these drugs on a child's brain became immediately evident when he first explained to us that Cooper's treatment would involve triaging the severity of his symptoms, and then trying to manage them—one at a time. Erik's sense of humor was the perfect match for Cooper and for us. From that first meeting in 2005 to this day, Erik's open nature made us feel like a team, always working together towards the same goals. His philosophical approach to medication was to administer the lowest dose possible that would yield the maximum benefit.

I especially appreciated that his caution was measured with reality. Each new drug required three to four weeks of titrating up to the therapeutic dose. If, by that time, there was no real benefit, or the drug created more problematic side effects than benefits, another three weeks were taken to wean off the medication. Many months are stolen from a child's life while working through a variety of cocktails to manage crippling symptoms, which can disappear just as mysteriously as they appear. Cooper displayed great courage and commitment for many years while enduring this malevolent vanishing act.

Steven and I hated these drugs; some pills were so huge that I couldn't believe Cooper could swallow them. And yet, it would have been irresponsible of us to idly watch as our son become prey to the symptoms that eroded his being, like watching a vulture pick the meat off a carcass. I discussed Steven's emerging concern about Cooper's pill-popping regimen with Dr. Erik. Steven was convinced that Cooper's potpourri of drugs would, in time, turn him into a drug addict.

"Patients who receive proper and effective medication therapy don't become drug addicts," Erik responded with calm certainty. I agreed with his conviction.

In third grade, the combination of constant tics, anti-depressants, and mood stabilizers resulted in Cooper regularly falling asleep in class.

He was almost always tired, and several times a week, the vice principal would call me to pick Cooper up from school early.

"You need to find a way to keep your son awake in class," she would reprimand me.

Right, I remember thinking, *I'll just shove a stick up his ass and move it up and down while his jack-in-the-box head bounces forward and back like a Slinky.*

I knew a smug response like that wouldn't have been appropriate, but couldn't she see how much it plagued me to have to pick up my son from school because he was too enervated to sit at his desk? Did she imagine that Cooper was immune to hurtful remarks from the kids making fun of him for snoring in class?

Cooper had lost much of his sparkle, but the drug combo reduced his motor tics. Finally he could sit in a chair again without falling to the floor from his body's violent jerks and thrusts. He even managed to get a spoonful of cereal and milk from the bowl into his mouth for breakfast—something he hadn't been able to do in previous months.

Wanting to eliminate the possibility of narcolepsy, Dr. Erik sent Cooper to St. John's Hospital for a sleep study. A technician placed dozens of electrodes on his head, body, legs, and arms. Cooper fell asleep fairly quickly, while I stayed in the bed in the next room. Fortunately, we learned that Cooper didn't have narcolepsy after all.

Erik began to prescribe Provigil for off-label use. Typically, this drug was used for narcolepsy, but it ended up being the only drug that helped Cooper remain alert without aggravating his tics. In the United States, each pill cost $10. I began buying Provigil on the Internet from a Canadian pharmacy for $1 per pill. I had discovered this alternative after four months of spending $1,200 dollars for just one of Cooper's five prescriptions. Six months passed before I got busted. I was notified by the Canadian pharmacy, per the United States Drug Enforcement Agency, that I could no longer buy drugs outside the United States by using a prescription over the Internet. Suddenly this was an illegal activity.

I was outraged. I wasn't going to let the pharmaceutical companies, the DEA, and the insurance company prevent me from helping my son and bankrupt me in the process. "Who the fuck are these people?" I wondered. "Why are they bothering with a sick young boy instead of going after the real drug lords?"

By this time, Dr. Erik had re-submitted a new request to Blue Cross, our insurance company, to cover Provigil, and he included Cooper's sleep study results with the paperwork. A Blue Cross insurance doctor reversed the denial of coverage, meaning we could move forward; but soon after, Cooper no longer needed to take the Provigil. I'm still haunted by the memory of that very long night of the sleep study, and how it was all just to get the insurance company to approve one drug to help my son after a documented trial of three previous drugs had failed him.

The avalanche of rejected Explanation of Benefits (EOBs) from our insurance company began to accumulate with our weekly mail delivery. The messages were often disappointing: some of the drugs prescribed by a highly respected neurologist to help my son were for off-label use and as such, were not covered by insurance, even though there were no alternative drugs approved for Cooper's comorbid symptoms from Tourette's, ADD, OCD, and a mood disorder. We were lucky, however; there happened to be a post office inside the pharmacy—which was rather convenient, considering the amount of time I spent mailing in re-submitted claims.

Regularly, I would call up the insurance company and try to defend why Dr. Erik prescribed a particular medication. After being sucked into the cyclone of voice mail hell, I would explain to an impatient or insensitive claims processor how we had exhausted all the other drugs in this class, either because they exacerbated other symptoms or simply didn't help. I tried to be respectful, but there I was, describing the effect of mood stabilizers and antipsychotics to a customer service representative who couldn't even pronounce the names of these generic compounds if she tried. The conversation always resulted in new forms that my doctor and I would need to complete in order for the claims to be re-submitted for approval. Of course, I would incur a new charge from our doctor each time, just for the privilege of giving my child additional attention.

This dysfunctional system forces you to think, to question authority. Had I been ignoring the uncovered medical claims, I would have easily amassed tens of thousands of dollars in medical bills. As it was, a tally close to $70,000 dollars per year in out-of-pocket medical costs quickly devoured my 401k savings. Steven and I often wondered who could possibly afford the cost for mental health care.

During occasional moments of reason, I was grateful for the resources available to us. It was in my nature to be an optimist and a problem solver. I've never been one who is easily embarrassed about asking stupid questions, so I asked plenty. My career as a music and licensing deal negotiator had taught me how to identify and leverage meaningful information, so I was a skilled researcher. I was also thankful for the lessons I had learned years earlier from working with Dr. Timothy Leary, the counterculture hero from the sixties, who always reiterated his confidence in my ability to "think for myself," and as a result, I accepted nothing at face value.

I had first met Timothy Leary in 1981 when he became one of my clients while I was still a booking agent in Los Angeles. He reminded me of Fingal the Fearless, a legendary Irish wizard, with his gray hair, ruddy skin, and bright-blue eyes, which conveyed a youthful mischievousness. I found his vivacious energy contagious.

"Let's shake things up, then, shall we?" he would always say with a devilish smile.

I vividly remember the shock and awe we created when I began to solicit a college lecture tour for Tim with his former nemesis, G. Gordon Liddy, the man who had invaded his home at gunpoint to bust him twice in the mid-1960s. Liddy later went to jail on charges from his involvement in the Watergate scandal. Two ex-cons together on the college lecture circuit. The motivation to do the tour was the guarantee: $10,000 dollars per night for each.

Early in Leary's research career, he made valuable contributions in understanding how interpersonal processes might facilitate diagnosing disorders and identifying human personality patterns. In the 1950s, he developed what is known as Leary's Circumflex, where every human trait can be mapped as a vector coordinate within this circle. A well-adjusted person could have their personality mapped at the exact center of the Circumflex; right at the intersection of the two axes, while individuals exhibiting extremes in personality would be located on the circumference of the circle.

Leary's profile had peaked in 1960, when Professor David McClelland invited him to join the Harvard Center for Research in Personality as the director of the Harvard Psilocybin Project. Leary was to analyze the effects of psilocybin on human subjects from a synthesized version of the drug LSD, which was still legal at the time. Psilocybin, an organic compound found in a variety of mushrooms from Mexico, is quickly metabolized by the body into psilocin and acts on serotonin receptors in the brain, resulting in a mind-altering experience similar to LSD.

Dr. Leary's first test subjects were thirty-six inmates from the Concord Prison in Massachusetts. The early results of this study indicated that the inmates who were administered therapy and LSD exhibited a reduction in recidivism versus those taking a placebo. However, things went awry in May of 1963, when the Harvard Corporation fired Leary and his cohort, Dr. Richard Alpert, now known as the spiritual teacher

Ram Dass. Alpert had been fired for giving LSD to undergraduates, while Leary was fired for failing to show up to teach his classes. In 1968 Leary moved to California, and soon after was faced with charges of marijuana possession. He was sent to prison from 1973 to 1976, and was regarded at the time as "the most dangerous man in America" by President Richard Nixon.

Timothy and I maintained contact over a span of twelve years. Sometimes we'd just bump into each other at Internet industry conventions, or cross paths as a result of mutual acquaintances. I was working at Rhino Entertainment in the '90s when I invited Timothy to talk about the future and the Internet as a featured lunchtime speaker. Seeming right at home in the Rhino conference room with thirty staffers huddled around to hear him, Leary stated, "The Internet is the LSD of the '90s." I thought then, as I do now, that Tim was a master in his understanding about our culture, society, and mass communication. His thoughts about the future included the next evolution of our species, our adoption of artificial intelligence, the similarity of the human brain and computers. That lunch was the last time we saw each other, as Tim passed away several years later.

Timothy will always be remembered for his motto, "Think for yourself. Question authority." When I first heard him say it, I couldn't have imagined then how much this iconic phrase would become my close companion and salvation while grappling with the mental health establishment. But I summon up this phrase as a personal mantra in circumstances that lack reason, when faced with a baffling diagnosis or rejected insurance claims. I use it when mental health laws like HIPAA sequester me from those I love, and for whom I am the caretaker. It has served me well, because when it comes to mental illness there are few answers, and we must all become advocates.

CHAPTER 6

TIC, SQUEAK, BREATHE...
DR. JOHN PIACENTINI

*What we need is more people who
specialize in the impossible.*
—THEODORE ROETHKE

In 1995, when I called my mother to tell her that I was pregnant with our second son, Cooper, she said, "Love multiplies." Having a child with OCD can sometimes take that sentiment to new heights. Monday through Friday at 7:45 a.m., just before leaving for school, Cooper and I would face each other near the front hallway, standing six feet apart. I'd blow him a kiss, which he'd catch with his hand and then rub on his chest. "If you ever need me, just put your hand on your heart," I'd often remind him. "You'll know I'm there." He would then return an air kiss to me, and we'd both exaggerate the physical demands of being a kiss pitcher or kiss catcher. He counted these kisses—serious business to Cooper—and we each had to have an equal amount before he left for school. If Steven, or Cooper's brother, Ben, innocently stepped between us during this ritual, however, his concentration would be derailed and he'd get flustered and angry and lose count of the number of kisses. We would have to go back to kiss one.

This ritual escalated over time until one morning I realized that I was hyperventilating attempting to quickly blow fifty air kisses before the school bus arrived. When I had to go out of town for business, Cooper would watch me blow fifty-one kisses into a ziplock bag, an extra kiss for good luck, and he'd save them in his backpack. These were emergency kisses; usually he wouldn't open the bag until I returned.

On the flip side of this ritual of sweetness waited a relentless torture. From the age of seven, Cooper had relied on a cocktail of drugs to get through a meal, to get through the day, to get through his childhood. Inside our kitchen cabinets was a pharmacy filled with rows of new and old pill bottles, refills of unopened prescriptions that were unsuccessful, and bottles of a drug with a variety of dose strengths, most of which were an unreliable solution for Cooper's complex mood, behavior, and motor and vocal tic symptoms. I spent an inordinate amount of time rearranging the bottles and pillboxes, these inanimate objects, as though by doing this I was somehow helping my son. I wasn't at all. Cooper was miserable.

Cooper's disability disabled our entire family as we witnessed his seemingly endless and erratic suffering. He was increasingly angry and frustrated at me for not anticipating—rather, for contributing to—his triggers, so I felt like I was always walking on eggshells in my own home. My life was crumbling, and I was becoming more isolated as I lived in a swirling vortex of chaos, rituals, and pills.

By the time Cooper was ten, he had already spent three years attempting to manage consistently unpredictable vocal and motor tics. I remember feeling helpless and desperate when he once went four months without a tic break—that's four months with a prominent tic presenting every ten seconds. The constant tics consumed an amount of energy equal to that of running daily marathons, so my child often looked sickly and languid. *He can't suffer like this for the rest of his life,* I thought. *No one could.* We needed help, and in a moment of synchronicity, my darkest fear collided into hope when I came upon a flier for a clinical trial.

I was on my way to get a mammogram when I saw the announcement on a bulletin board by the elevator in the medical building about a CBIT Study taking place. The Childhood OCD, Anxiety, and Tic Disorders Program at UCLA's Neuropsychiatric Institute (NPI) was recruiting children with tic disorders for a clinical trial. I had no idea what CBIT meant, which was strange, since just about anything involving the treatment of childhood OCD, anxiety, and tics would have already been on my radar. The words *clinical trial* suggested that a cutting-edge therapy was involved. I wrote down the contact number and when I got home, I called to learn more about the study.

CBIT, it turned out, stood for cognitive behavior intervention therapy. Unlike the intervention with Aerosmith, this intervention was about habit reversal training and tic-awareness training. I didn't really understand how a child could develop power over involuntary, random, determined tics. I had seen Cooper try to sit on his hands to prevent his arms from flailing; ultimately, he ended up spewing vocal tics and breaking any nearby object, a pencil or a spoon, for example. I had seen him try to control spit tics—where he would spit his saliva across the room, on the carpet—by biting on the neck of his T-shirt. I wished more than anything that Cooper could stop being at the mercy of his tics, and that he could change his brain and gain some control over his body. I signed up for a screening appointment for the trial and was told that if he were selected, Cooper would be paid $175 for participating in and completing the study, a nice payout for a ten-year-old.

I knew Cooper wasn't going to be placid spending three hours in yet another doctor's office answering questions after an already harrowing day at school. His tics, and the ongoing explanations they required, had become an annoyance and an embarrassment for him. When at school, he hid behind his glasses and long, brown bangs, often holding his head low, avoiding eye contact. He didn't want to be seen.

On the day of the interview, I decided to pick him up during lunch so he could come home early, change his clothes, and have a break before going to UCLA. He was exceedingly ticcy, constantly blinking his eyes, a gesture exaggerated by his extremely long eyelashes. The tics made his lashes flutter and drag against his eyeglass lenses like broken windshield wipers. Meanwhile, the neck of his T-shirt had holes from the bite marks he'd made trying to suppress the spit tics.

After picking him up, I broke the silence in the car and said, "Coop, guess what?"

"Ww-what?" he asked from the back seat.

"Dad and I think you should be paid for your time at UCLA today."

"Yy-yes! *Squeak-squeak-squeak.* How mm-much?"

"Five bucks sound pretty good?"

He nodded. "Jj-just for gg-going *squeak-squeak squeak* to UCLA?" Cooper was no stranger to UCLA. His neurologist had an office in UCLA Medical Plaza.

"This is different, Boo. Today you'll be spending time answering a lot of questions for an important research study that could help you and other kids with Tourette's."

Cooper no longer seemed excited. He was in the midst of a tic flurry, a phase of non-stop involuntary vocal and motor tics. He agreed to go, however, and we drove to the OCD, Anxiety, and Tic Disorders clinic.

When we stepped through the door, we heard a welcoming voice say, "Hi! You must be Cooper!" I was so grateful for the kindness of the intake coordinator, Michelle Rozenman, and I was operating on blind faith that as long as we kept moving ahead, we'd find help. Michelle showed us to a private room, gave me a stack of paperwork, and gave Cooper a wrapped package of cheese and crackers—one of his favorite snacks.

"Don't forget," she reminded us, "there will be two groups in the study. One group will receive therapy and learn about Tourette's; the other group will learn habit reversal intervention. This is a random study, which means that if you get accepted, you cannot tell anyone—not the investigators, not even me—which group you're in."

"We understand," I answered, desperately wanting for Cooper to get into the habit-reversal group.

Michelle smiled. "You guys are set. Just fill out the forms, and Dr. Piacentini will be in shortly." Michelle left the room and closed the door behind her.

Dr. John Piacentini was Chief of Child Psychology at the UCLA Semel Institute, Professor of Psychiatry at the UCLA School of Medicine, and Director of the Child OCD, Anxiety, and Tic Disorders Program; Chair of the Behavioral Sciences Consortium of the Tourette Association of America, and he was the lead investigator for the CBIT clinical trial.

The parent forms were primarily for consent and indemnification, while Cooper's paperwork, which required my help, was a lengthy questionnaire for him to identify his tics, and also rate the frequency, interference, and severity of each one. After fifteen minutes of working my way down Cooper's forms and circling the number 5 for the frequency of each tic he had on the list, I sensed something unusual.

"Coop," I whispered, concealing my mouth with my hand. "Look at these windows. I think they might be observation windows. Maybe someone's watching us."

"May-be, *grunt-grunt-squeak*," he replied with a shrug.

Just in case, I adjusted my posture and tried to look more composed and confident than I felt. If we were being observed, I wanted them to see a loving and supportive mother. I knew the study was recruiting kids between the ages of nine and seventeen, which would place Cooper among the youngest if he got in. They wouldn't choose a misbehaving younger child if they could work with a more mature child with Tourette's instead, nor would they waste their time on a dysfunctional, defensive family. We needed to exhibit our commitment to working hard throughout the study, and to guarantee that Cooper would have unconditional support on the home front. I wanted them to see respect and responsibility so that we could be relied upon to fulfill whatever would be required of us. Because of this, I almost panicked when I saw the mess Cooper was making with his snack.

"Mmm, *squeak-squeak-squeak* those crackers were good," Cooper said, smiling with cracker crumbs clinging to his lips and wedged in between his fingers. "*Squeak-grunt-grunt* I'm thirsty now."

I spotted a box of tissues in the office and handed it to Cooper. "Wipe around your mouth and clean up, okay? There's a trashcan behind you."

Cooper pulled most of the tissues out of the box, which was an OCD trait. One napkin or one tissue was never adequate because the top one was considered used, and the ones behind it contained germs.

If Cooper was being observed, surely they would see a kind and thoughtful child, betrayed by the involuntary and uncomfortable gesticulations of his body. "*Please help him,*" I prayed silently. "*Please release him from so much suffering.*" Why was I praying in a doctor's office? Anyone who could help my son was already God-like to me.

There was a knock, and then the door opened.

"Hi, I'm sorry you had to wait," greeted the man in the shirt and tie standing in the doorway. He exuded youthfulness, except for a few facial lines and graying hair near his temples. "I'm John Piacentini."

"Hello," I began, and then blurted out: "You look so much younger than your photo on the NPI website." I couldn't believe that was the first thing I said to him, but I was too stressed and anxious to think clearly. "Thank you for considering Cooper for the trial," I said. "He's been on meds for over two years, and at best it's like a game of real-life Whack-A-Mole."

"I understand," he replied. He was empathetic to my pleas for help, which I found very comforting. "The typical treatment for reducing tic severity is antipsychotic medications such as haloperidol and risperidone," he continued, "but they rarely eliminate tics and are often associated with unacceptable sedation, weight gain, cognitive dulling, and adverse motor effects."

I nodded. Finally, here was someone who understood what we had already been through, and what we were looking for. Piacentini paused to observe Cooper's vocal and motor tics.

"*Spit...grunt-squeak-squeak.*" Cooper tried to hold in a full body tic, which caused his chair to move, the metal legs sounding like a lame horse wobbling against the linoleum floor.

Dr. Piacentini explained that the trial was designed to evaluate the efficacy of a comprehensive behavioral intervention for tics based on habit reversal training, as well as reducing tics and tic-related impairment in a large sample of children and adolescents with Tourette's. UCLA was one of three study sites; the other two were Johns Hopkins in Baltimore and the University of Wisconsin-Milwaukee. The investigators at each clinical site were collaborating with researchers at Yale University, Massachusetts General Hospital/Harvard Medical School, and the University of Texas.

My heart raced with excitement. We had stumbled into the first and largest clinical study to treat Tourette's using behavioral therapy. This was an important study, and I was desperate for Cooper to be included. This was it; this was his big chance.

"If Cooper gets into the study, he'll meet with a therapist eight times over a ten-week period," he said. "The first two sessions are ninety minutes long, and a parent or guardian will need to be here to participate."

"That won't be a problem, Dr. Piacentini," I said. "My husband or I will be here—*I'll* be here." For the sake of consistency, I decided that if Cooper got into the study, I'd be his partner in crime. After all, signing him up had been my big idea, and the trial would be time-intensive. I was able and willing to make the investment, schlepping back and forth to UCLA each week in rush hour traffic. I wanted this for Cooper and I would be undeterred—even if it meant flying up Westwood Boulevard on broomsticks or saddling up the two mastiffs that lived in our neighborhood. Whatever it took, we would be at UCLA.

Dr. Piacentini smiled and went on to explain that participants in each group would receive therapy, working one-on-one with a trained therapist.

"Can you explain what the kids in the habit reversal group will be doing?" I asked, seeking to understand the bottom-line benefit of the trial.

Piacentini looked at Cooper. "Have you ever tried to hold in your tics?

"Yes," Cooper answered. "I can hold them back *squeak-squeak-grunt* for a little time, but then they have to come out."

"How do you feel when you hold them in?"

"Bad and mad," Cooper replied. "*Squeak-squeak-grunt.* I can't pay attention in school."

"Good," Piacentini replied, turning back to me. "During that time when he's holding in his tics, we think that this awareness opens the possibility to behavior modification. By introducing an intervention or a competing response, the patient experiences less anxiety and, ultimately, a reduction of tics."

I thanked Dr. Piacentini for his time and for considering Cooper for the study. By now, I didn't care how pathetic I might seem. I was willing to do anything—I would ask Michelle if she needed a slave to help stuff envelopes; I'd try to raise more money for the Tourette Association, or find a board member to call Dr. Piacentini on our behalf. Yes, I was desperate, and, if necessary, I was prepared to beg our way into this trial.

After we got home, Cooper walked into my office sobbing. He plopped down into the oversized green chair. I turned to give him my full attention.

"Cooper, what happened?" I asked, looking at the sorrow on his face, an expression of overwhelming rejection and isolation.

"Why doesn't God love me?" he cried with his head held down low. The only sound in the quiet of my office were his large teardrops as they slowly dripped, one by one, and landed on the wood floor.

A lump in my throat pained and silenced me, holding back my tears like the tension of a dike about to burst. In three years, Cooper had never expressed self-pity, had never asked, "Why me?"

"Cooper," I began, "God loves you, or you wouldn't be here to be loved." Kneeling in front of the chair, I hugged him with every molecule of love flowing through my body. "I will always have your back and I will never give up. And you can never give up because I know if we keep trying, something good will happen."

I felt his damp face on my neck as he nodded his head.

When Michelle called several days later to inform us that Cooper had an appointment to start the ten-week program, my bruised and beaten soul exploded with emotion and renewed purpose. We wouldn't be fighting this demon alone. We were now part of a collaborative community as vested in helping our son as we were.

Cooper's reaction: "I'm gonna *squeak-squeak* be rich!"

The first two sessions were long, an hour and a half each. During the first hour, Cooper and the investigator went into an office and reviewed a checklist of all the tics he had experienced in the past week. Cooper then rated the current motor and vocal tics on a severity scale of one to five. He'd rate each tic based on frequency, intensity, complexity, and interference. I would remain outside the office, sitting on the floor in the corridor working on the Parent Tic Questionnaire. My form listed twenty-eight motor and vocal tics to be marked as present or absent during the past week, and I was also expected to rate the tics that were present on a severity scale between one and four. During the last half-hour, I joined Cooper in the office, and one-by-one, the investigator compared my assessments to Cooper's to establish consistency.

These tic assessments were the worst part of the study. Cooper had so many tics, some of which wouldn't even stop until he fell asleep at night. Focusing on each tic from the previous week and rating them was tedious, exhausting, and frustrating for both of us. This was usually when Cooper displayed his anger, telling me to shut up, or swatting at me with his lifeless, tired arm. He'd slide out of his chair onto the floor and complain about wanting to leave. I would put on a brave face because, after all, the sessions were video-recorded. No one would know Cooper's name, but the tape would be shared with the Tourette Syndrome Behavioral Consortium, the team of researchers, investigators, members of the NIMH, and the CDC, which funded the five-year study.

The big reveal was week three, during our session with Dr. Eunice Kim, when Cooper realized that he was in the competing response, habit-reversal training group. Dr. Kim was young, kind, and intelligent, and Cooper knew that he wouldn't be judged during their sessions. This was the one place where he was encouraged to exhibit and discuss his tics, the one place in the world where he didn't have to try to hide them.

Dr. Kim explained, and Cooper confirmed, that he could feel a premonitory urge, usually in his chest area, just before a tic. The tic awareness assessments were essential to helping Cooper learn how to self-monitor these urges. Step 1 was for Cooper to learn how to recognize the urge to tic. Step 2 was to learn new, voluntary behaviors that were physically incompatible with the tic. Finally, Step 3 was to replace the urge with the new behavior and prevent the tic from happening instead of trying to suppress it once it got going.

Dr. Kim and Cooper developed a tic hierarchy and ranked his tics from most to least distressing. For Cooper, the first tic they worked on was what he called the "full body tic." I called it "Mousetrap." In a nanosecond, a brisk tic in his rib cage would trigger his arm to thrust upward and then sharply collapse by his side; his shoulder would swiftly jut up to his ear, which caused his neck to jerk. In that brief, rapid moment, it looked as though his head and shoulder were connected. The position of his torso appeared out of alignment, like the top of Gumby's head. Then it seemed like the tic was sending a signal to his right leg until it kicked out to the side, looking almost like the rapid leg propulsion of the frog stroke. This was his most noticeable tic, and competing response therapy would allow him to ease into a more socially acceptable posture.

Towards the end of the first therapy session, Dr. Kim asked me into the office. "Okay, Cooper, let's show your mom." She then instructed Cooper to look forward, with his arms by his side, his chin slightly tucked down while gently tensing his neck muscles for sixty seconds.

I watched in complete amazement. Cooper barely ticced for almost a full minute! He looked a bit awkward, stiff, and robotic, but the basic concept worked. My heart was bursting with happiness because for the first time in nearly four months, Cooper finally had a break, a minute of calm. His mind was in control of his body, and if he could do it once, he could do it again with practice. "I'm so proud of you, Cooper!" I exclaimed. "It looks hard, but you did it!"

"Competing responses requires a lot of concentration and practice," Dr. Kim explained. A few seconds later, when he felt another tic coming on, Cooper went into position without hesitation.

"You did it on your own, Cooper!" Dr. Kim cheered. She seemed both surprised and excited to see Cooper wholeheartedly embracing this therapy. "I want you to use your competing responses at school and at home."

At the end of the first therapy session, parents rated their expectations about whether their child's assigned treatment would have a benefit. I wrote down a rating of four, but in my heart, it was a five. Seeing the expression on Cooper's face, filled with determination and understanding that he could exert control over his brain and his body, was a sight I couldn't have imagined the day before.

Each week, Dr. Kim would ask Cooper how much time he'd spent working on his competing responses, the situations in which he was successful, and when it didn't seem to work. As Cooper's coach, I had to encourage him to practice. To avoid embarrassing him in public, we agreed that, when necessary, I'd quietly say, "PE," our code for "practice your exercises."

During the next session, I watched as Dr. Kim and Cooper worked on vocal tics...*squeaky*, *barky*, and *grunty*. Slow, rhythmic breathing from the diaphragm for sixty seconds was the competing response. Dr. Kim placed her hand on Cooper's belly to make sure that his stomach filled with air on the inhale and deflated on the exhale.

"This one is good for him to practice in bed at night," she explained. "It will help loosen and relax his muscles from being pulled throughout the day."

"I can help with that," I said with confidence. I hadn't meditated since college when I practiced transcendental meditation to help with my cluster headaches, and now I realized how much I had missed it. Although the breathing was different, the relaxation benefit was similar.

By the end of these sessions, Cooper had a new friend in Dr. Kim and a new coach in me. Cooper and I were going to miss Dr. Kim. We had become a team, and she had been an integral part of his healing. Cooper offered to buy her frozen yoghurt at Penguin's with the money he earned from the study, an idea which she loved.

After ten weeks, Cooper experienced a reduction in tic frequency, but the tough work was in the months ahead. At home, when the environment seemed less anxious, I worked with him on his competing responses, but school wasn't an adaptable place for him to focus on his exercises.

Still, Cooper was having a better time of coping with his affliction. Just before the holidays, Cooper asked me to take him to the mall to buy gifts for his teachers. He had been wearing a long-sleeved jersey and jeans, and I noticed that he had pulled his right arm out of his shirt. The empty sleeve flapped and swayed like one of those blow-up figures you see in front of mattress stores or outside of a used car lot during a sale.

"Cooper, where's your arm?" I knew where it was, I just didn't understand why he was hiding it.

He inched up the bottom front of his jersey and waved his fingertips.

"Why did you take your arm out of your sleeve? It looks kind of goofy," I said affectionately.

Cooper whispered, "Don't turn around, but there's a *squeak-squeak-grunt* little boy behind us. He won't say anything about my *spit-squeak-squeak* tics. He'll say, 'Mom, look at the poor kid with one arm!'"

As if on cue, we heard this loud-mouthed voice shout, "Look, Mama! See that boy? He only has one arm!"

The mother shushed her boy, and then sighed, "Poor child." She briskly walked past us while clutching her son, which made us laugh even harder.

I smiled at Cooper. His long, caramel-colored hair was hiding his face, but his shoulders were moving up and down from chuckling. Light, happy moments were so infrequent and unexpected that I didn't realize how much time we'd spent in the mall. The thirty-minute errand mark was Cooper's limit, and I realized a bit too late that we had pushed his patience. We were now headed for an explosion of exhaustion, frustration, and tic escalation.

I stopped, looked at Cooper, and in a low, firm voice said, "PE." Cooper stopped next to me, both arms tensing by his side, chin down, neck muscles taut, as his diaphragm filled with air. He did this repeatedly for sixty seconds. *Dr. John Piacentini is a rock star!* I thought, as I marveled at how well CBIT was working, right there in the Westside Mall! I so wanted to hug Cooper with all of my might, but instead I patiently waited for him to finish his exercise.

"Wasn't that good?" Cooper asked, positively glowing and proud of this huge accomplishment. "But you have to do me a favor," he added. "I'm tired and I need to yell, so we have to leave right now! I can wait until we get in the car, but you have to promise to close the door the second we get inside. Understand?" It was stressful and draining living with Attila the Hun. Cooper hadn't developed patience, and his requests sounded like commands.

I had no choice but to agree, and as soon as we got in the car, there was a deafening scream. Cooper was able to express his rage in an appropriate place and warn me beforehand so I wouldn't freak out. Although my ears were ringing, Cooper had articulated a reasonable way for him to channel his frustration. This was the first time in over a year that Cooper didn't melt down in public. Crazy as it may sound, I was so very proud of his restraint.

Several nights later, Cooper asked me to help him with his exercises. He had never before elicited my help. It was only 7:00 p.m., but he was ready to go to sleep. He took me by the hand and told his dad and his brother that we had to practice breathing. He explained that once he closed his bedroom door, they couldn't come in or interrupt us—"No matter what!"

Cooper got into his bed and under the sheets. I turned off his light and positioned myself next to him, head to toe on top of the bed. In a soft, meditative voice, I began: "I want you to find a comfortable position. Place your arms beside you, and your legs long and relaxed. Close your eyes."

I waited several seconds until we both seemed comfortable.

"In a few minutes, we're going to take three very deep breaths. When you breathe in, expand your stomach into a big balloon with so much air you feel as though you might fly away. We'll hold that to the count of five, then exhale slowly until your stomach is flat again, OK?"

"Okay," Cooper whispered.

"Breathe in, and hold for 60 seconds. Now, gently, slowly breathe out." You could hear our release, "Phew."

"Your body feels so comfortable, so relaxed, and so weightless, like floating on clouds."

We began with our head muscles, then our temples, neck, shoulders, arms, and down to our hips.

"Okay, now we're going to do three more really deep breaths, and try to hold each one for 60 seconds."

We continued moving down our bodies; our spine, and abdomen, to our legs and toes.

This was the first of nearly 180 consecutive nights of Cooper and me, alone in the quiet of his room, doing our breathing exercises together. Sometimes it would take twenty minutes, sometimes thirty minutes. I made certain to continue until he stopped ticking, which meant he was asleep. Some nights were especially hard for me. My son was a sweet, intelligent, loveable child, but the exterior could be a volatile, foul-mouthed, tic-ravaged boy. There had been many nights when I'd try to suck in breaths so deep in an attempt to inhale Cooper's Tourette's until it left his body. I felt like Grendel's mother, rising up from the vapors to save her son from Beowulf, the beast. However, neither Grendel's mother nor I could alter our sons' fate. During the last month of our nightly breathing ritual, I'd become so relaxed and cozy being with Cooper that I'd fall asleep, faintly hearing, "Mum, Mummy, are you awake?"

The clinical trial lasted three months, followed by a three-month "tune-up" and a final follow-up six months later. It was a transformative experience for not only me, but for Cooper, who learned he could have some control over his body. Throughout the yearlong timeline of the study, Cooper had many tic-free days—time he lived without physical limitations, playing in the basketball league with his friends. I will always be grateful to Dr. Piacentini for accepting Cooper into the study. If not for him, Cooper wouldn't have had this wonderful excerpt of normal, joyful days, which filled his brain cells with some positive childhood memories.

During our last session with Dr. Kim, she showed us a longitudinal graph of childhood onset Tourette's, which tends to intensify before puberty and diminish somewhat by age sixteen. Often, symptoms remit by age nineteen through adulthood. I believe this was meant to give us even more hope, but unfortunately, Cooper's worst years were yet to come.

CHAPTER 7

THIS IS NOT MY BEAUTIFUL HOUSE...*DR. ROSS GREENE*

There is no pain so great as the
memory of joy in present grief.
—AESCHYLUS

A corporate consolidation at Bertelsmann Music Group resulted in me receiving a two-year contract payout, but I was on my own in terms of paying for health insurance coverage for my family and me. Money for expensive drugs and specialists gushed out of our savings so quickly, as if it were pouring out of a broken spigot that we couldn't turn off. Challenging authority became a way of life for me and I was determined to find a health insurance provider without pre-existing exclusions for Cooper's Tourette's and Ben's panic attacks and anxiety. Our mental health specialists were all out of network, and most doctors, hospitals, and lab fee charges in West Los Angeles exceeded the approved national average cost for services. Health insurance premiums were very high, and mental health reimbursements were capped at 50 percent of the national average cost for the service. *Whoever contracted those rates erroneously presumed that Los Angeles was Beverly Hills, 90210.*

Soon our savings would be depleted, I projected, and we'd have to sell our house and move to the Deep South, someplace near Appalachia, where the standard of living was less expensive. Yet, moving wasn't a great option because Cooper needed a stable environment; relocation and the stress of a move would ultimately escalate his condition. I was beginning to fear that obtaining good mental health insurance was unattainable—until Candy Newberry came into our lives.

Candy is a medical insurance broker for individuals and small businesses. One of Steven's partners suggested I contact her. She drove to our house from Anaheim one morning and spent hours helping us make sense of our debacle, proposing several scenarios that would best meet our health insurance coverage needs. After Dr. Erik, she became the second member of our A-team. Per her guidance, Steven and I met with our attorney to form a business LLC, which would guarantee small group insurance coverage for the boys without any pre-existing exclusions. This was a huge victory for our family.

Candy also helped me get organized. To help keep track of things, I created my own bible: two inch-thick, three-ring Staples binders containing copies of monthly medication and titration charts from Dr. Erik; pediatric physical results relating to dramatic weight gain or loss from medications; blood test results; my notes about any new symptoms that may have emerged; the month's most problematic school and family issues; and finally, rejected medical insurance claims forms.

These administrative issues showcased my competencies but my self-esteem waned, the result of new battles to wage at every turn. There were teachers who suspected Cooper of having Oppositional Defiant Disorder (ODD), because they didn't understand how similar those symptoms could be to Attention Deficit Disorder (ADD), and they failed to discipline him in constructive ways. Cooper would explain that he couldn't do his homework; which they, as did I, initially believed meant he *wouldn't* do it. After-school detention, during which he had to sit still at his desk for an hour, was an ineffective punishment for this crime.

I had thought that Cooper's tortured life couldn't get much worse, until ...*BUM, BUM, BUM, BUM*...Coprolalia—Cooper's involuntary burst of: "*Motherfuckingbitch-cunt-nigger-cunt-nigger-cunt.*" This expression rarely escaped his lips as a scream; the tonal range for these outbursts was somewhere between a loud whisper to a typical speaking voice.

Cooper had come home from school one afternoon and told me that his teacher, Ray, recommended he try saying other words like "runt," and "trigger." Ray didn't comprehend or believe that uttering this string of heinous words wasn't Cooper's choice.

"Does Ray honestly think I haven't already tried?" Cooper was bewildered, as his voice struggled to hide yet another sense of defeat. His tears were filled with desperate alienation from not being understood. "Does he really think so little of me?" he asked. "Mom, you know that I would never want to say these words." Yes, of course I knew, but apparently too few others did.

This ongoing torment was too cruel, so unjust, and I wept, imagining Cooper's profound misery. Coprolalia encompasses the most culturally taboo words or phrases, and is not a reflection of one's belief's or thoughts. I once read that the chance of having coprolalia increases linearly with the number of comorbid conditions: patients with four or five other conditions—in addition to tics—were four to six times more likely to have coprolalia than persons with only Tourette's.

I remember mustering what remained of my positive attitude, thinking, *Okay, this new symptom, like the other vocal tics, will run its course; things have to get better.* Then I panicked. Cooper's school principal was a beautiful black woman and no one—including her—could possibly be that understanding. Regardless of what made Cooper say these words, they were too hurtful to hear. I couldn't expect anyone to discard the venom and understand they were said without malice or intent. Coprolalia, like all the other Tourette's-related conditions, waxed and waned, as did Cooper's school attendance for several months.

Fortunately, the worst of the coprolalia seemed to slowly diminish with time and a medication adjustment. Still, I couldn't have imagined symptoms that could wreak more devastation in our lives; until the unexplained and unexpected explosiveness, rage, and violence—worse than any foe yet—transformed my son into a beast, a Tasmanian devil.

Nightly battles began with shouts, "I can't do my homework!" and escalated into hours of uninterrupted screams. Cooper's after-school ritual became predictable, as did the cavalcade of flying objects crashing against his bedroom walls and into furniture: pencils, an electric sharpener, textbooks, spiral-bound notebooks, cups, basketball trophies, and other desk artifacts. Many nights Cooper's tics were so severe that he couldn't even hold a pencil to write.

The school administrators finally provided Cooper with a 504-education plan; Section 504 of the Rehabilitation Act of the 1973 federal civil rights law prohibits discrimination against public school students with disabilities. Eventually, the next member of our A-team, our Advocate, Elissa Henkin, petitioned the district for Cooper to receive an individual education plan (IEP) based on his other health-impaired (OHI) obstacles resulting from his unrelenting tics. A student with learning or attention issues, and who meets the criteria, receives adjustments and/or modifications, which are meant to remove barriers to learning.

Cooper's IEP included dictating his answers for assignments to a classmate at school or a teaching assistant. His attention was limited at night, partly because his stamina was spent from his day at school, so his math homework was modified. He was expected to complete only even-numbered math problems, just enough for the teachers to see that he grasped the curriculum.

When necessary, I would scribe for Cooper at home. During this time, when he seemed totally stuck, he'd ask for my help. At first, things would be calm, and he'd explain the assignment to me. After ten or twelve minutes, he would then be fuming with frustration, shouting, "I CAN'T DO THIS!" He would pound my arm with his fist, or jam his foot deep into my thigh and gouge my skin with his toenail. I couldn't take this abuse, and I would promptly leave the room.

"I'm so sorry, Mum, *cunt-fuckingnigger* please, I didn't mean *nigger-cunt* to hurt you," he'd sniffle over and over until I made it into my bedroom and closed the door behind me. Eventually, Cooper retreated to his room, homework incomplete. Steven would later follow me into our bedroom and would hold me as I cried myself to sleep. I too had feelings, and I was done with this homework insanity. I had plenty of family issues to manage—Cooper and his teachers would need to resolve schoolwork problems.

Around this time, my parents had already planned to stay with us for two weeks and I, bereft of a clear mind, never gave a thought about the timing of their visit. The last five years in our home were filled with anything but serenity, and I mindlessly included Cooper's new symptoms as part of our current landscape.

My father had an ebullient, sometimes over-the-top personality, and a tendency to be loud. He was so much fun, but unfortunately, during this trip, he was too much stimulation for Cooper to handle. One night, my parents were watching television in the den while I was setting the table for dinner. Out of nowhere, Cooper stampeded into the dining room, pushed me, spit at me, and hollered, "*YOU-CUNT-NIGGERCUNT!*" His face was red as he screamed and yelled.

The silverware *clinked* and *clanked* down onto the floor and land-ed with great emphasis. Cooper stomped back into his room shouting, "SHUT-UP-cuntnigger! Nigger-SHUT-UP!" before slamming his bedroom door so hard it made the house shake.

"Hurry, honey, quick!" I heard my father holler to my mother in ter-ror. "I think it's an earthquake!" My father hoisted my legally blind moth-er off the couch, grabbed her cane and shoved it into her hand. I never imagined that my mother could move so fast, and watched with grief as they ran under the front door jamb to safety.

"You're okay, guys," I said, and then tried to calmly motion for them to sit down. "I'm so sorry. Cooper slammed his door, and it shook the house."

My parents were utterly horrified at what they had witnessed; their own grandson's tempestuous behavior and, as my mother called it, "his filthy mouth." I foolishly hadn't considered that this phase of Cooper's rage, so familiar to me, would be shocking to my 78-year-old parents, who couldn't understand that Cooper was unable to hear anything dur-ing these tumultuous outbursts. Any attempt to respond with a typical parental admonition like, "Your behavior is unacceptable. No computer for two nights," would only escalate the madness.

Usually, when my parents would visit us from Boston and stay in our house, it was a treat. However, in this new phase of Cooper's affliction, there was no way that I could enlist my parents' support for his verbal abuse and behavior. They couldn't possibly embrace the notion that a spanking or a time-out wouldn't teach Cooper what he needed to learn.

I explained to my parents that I had to wait for Cooper to be calm before I'd go into his room and address his behavior. I reminded them about how several weeks before they arrived, Cooper had hurled one of my cherry wood dining room chairs into the wall. I pointed to the gap-ing hole and the pile of chipped yellow paint and plaster on the floor.

This resulted when I tried to interrupt a previous rage attack with typical parental discipline.

I had finally gained some insight into Cooper's rage and inflexibility after reading a book by Dr. Ross Greene, *The Explosive Child*. Screaming back at an inflexible, explosive child who was clearly in meltdown mode would only have catastrophic results...because it always had before. No, punitive parenting never worked before, and I knew that it wouldn't work now.

A seasoned professional, Dr. Greene has held positions in the Department of Psychiatry at Harvard Medical School and the school psychology program in the Department of Education at Tufts University. Greene founded the non-profit organization Lives in the Balance, a website for researchers, educators, and parents to further the understanding and adoption of Greene's therapy called Collaborative & Proactive Solutions, CPS. The site offers live, monthly question-and-answer sessions with leading behavior specialists from around the country.

In the July 2015 issue of *Mother Jones*, Katherine Reynolds Lewis interviewed Dr. Ross Greene in an article called, "What If Everything You Knew About Disciplining Kids Was Wrong?"

"The children at risk of falling into the school-to-prison pipeline,"
Greene says, "include not only the 5.2 million with ADHD, the 5
million with a learning disability, and the 2.2 million with anxiety
disorders, but also the 16 million who have experienced repeated
trauma or abuse, the 1.4 million with depression, the 1.2 million
on the autism spectrum, and the 1.2 million who are homeless."
He continues, "Not only are we not helping, we are going about
doing things in ways that make things worse. Then what you
have to show for it is a whole lot of alienated, hopeless, some-
times aggressive, sometimes violent kids."

The Explosive Child is the essential book for learning how to parent easily frustrated, inflexible, hypersensitive children. However, Greene's approach was, for us, much harder than a Parenting 101 class. Steven and I had to forget the logic and intuition we followed in parenting Ben. At first, working with Greene's model seemed counterintuitive—after all, we're the parents, and children had to be taught how to behave. But when rewards and punishments didn't incentivize Cooper to change his behavior, we had nothing to lose by trying Greene's CPS.

First, Steven and I had to create a user-friendly environment, one in which our parenting goals had to be carefully prioritized. We put an emphasis on reducing the overall demands for flexibility, keeping mindful of Cooper's frustration tolerance, because he'd already proven beyond a doubt that he didn't have the bandwidth to handle all of these frustrations. The number one behavioral issue we had to eradicate was Cooper's violence. The family's first priority was safety. Our second priority was Cooper's inappropriate language, and teaching him how language is connected to self-respect and respecting others. Greene's theory is that by reducing the opportunities for vapor lock and meltdowns, Cooper may become more successful in handling the frustration. One of the most important components for a user-friendly environment was to make certain that the adults who interacted with Cooper had a clear understanding of his unique difficulties, including the specific factors that fueled his inflexibility-explosiveness.

Greene's premise is that explosive kids *would* do well if they *could*, if they had developed the skills critical to being flexible, adaptive, and tolerant with frustration. I knew that Cooper didn't choose to be explosive and noncompliant, and despite everything, he always had a kind and soulful heart. It wasn't that he was unmotivated to be successful or unwilling to behave with reason; the problem was that some of the nerve cells in his brain misfired, and the transmitters didn't take those signals to the receptors.

Cooper's impairment resided in the prefrontal cortex of his brain, which is associated with executive thinking skills, a deficit that is extremely common in kids with ADD, ADHD, and OCD. It wasn't natural for Cooper to ease into mental transitions, organize his thoughts, or control his impulses because he still needed help in developing those skills. As Greene explains in his book, the goal is identifying and limiting triggers on the front end, and to do this in collaboration with Cooper. This way Cooper was still in control of his life, and in time, he would understand that I was on his side, too. Unfortunately, anticipating triggers on the front end can't always be accommodated.

For example, Dr. Greene might have suggested a more effective parenting scenario, in which Cooper and I would have discussed the best way for him to deal with my parents' upcoming visit.

"What can we do so you can be okay when Gramsie and Papa stay with us?" I would ask in this scenario. "I know Papa's loud voice can be annoying and really distracting."

Cooper would have appreciated that I had considered and understood how hard the overstimulation might be for him. We'd agree that Papa means well, but his animated personality added to Cooper's anxiety, especially after a stressful day at school. I'd stand firm with my desire to have my parents visit me in my home for a few weeks, but offer alternatives to reduce the added frustration of my father being in Cooper's space. Perhaps we wouldn't have solved this problem right away, but at least Cooper would have known I understood how tough the situation would be on him.

What happened instead was that, upon simply walking past my parents to go to his room to begin his homework, Cooper became instantly distracted, fixating on my father's loud laugh. Cooper went into his room and as he was sitting at his desk, distracted beyond reason, and unable to do his homework, his rage escalated, leading to his outburst and the mistaken earthquake that followed. After assaulting me, Cooper stayed in his room that night, only emerging to grab something to eat from the fridge. He then returned to his room, ticcing and whimpering until he fell asleep.

My parents left several days later and we all felt discouraged, disappointed, and saddened by what would be my mother's last visit before she died. I, however, continued walking on eggshells, willing to avoid anything that could trigger Cooper's still highly combustible behavior. Days later, I caught Cooper in a more open and less anxious mood, and we talked about what we could both do next time to avoid him going into meltdown.

Of course, to my parents, and especially to Ben, it seemed as though Cooper never received consequences for his bad behavior. Admittedly, it would be several years before I became comfortable and more effective with discipline strategies for Cooper. There was still a part of me that felt Cooper's punishment was in knowing that something inside his brain made it impossible for him to be around us at times.

A new dimension of Cooper's uber-sensitivity was his acute sense of smell. Early on, we all found it hard to believe that specific smells and sounds could trigger fierce rage spirals; but Cooper always knew when, hours earlier, for example, I had chewed bubble gum in the car. He could always smell when someone had eaten a breath mint. From upstairs he could sense when someone was downstairs in the kitchen "schmatzing," like the sound of eating a banana. He'd follow us around the house with his jersey pulled up over his mouth and nose and beg us, plead with us, not to chew gum or eat anything minty, or schmatzy food like peanut butter or bananas.

By the time he had turned 14 years old, he accurately self-diagnosed misophonia, which means hatred of sound; he actually has selective sound sensitivity syndrome, which is linked to Tourette's. Most people with misophonia are commonly angered by specific sounds, such as slurping, gum chewing or snapping, laughing, humming, whistling, or singing. TV celebrity Kelly Ripa came out as being amongst the afflicted. Sufferers experience fight/flight symptoms such as sweating, muscle tension, and quickened heartbeat. Eating at the table together, as a family, or even going out to dinner together was eliminated in 2010.

Adopting the Ross Greene user-friendly environment meant compromising and considering the needs and desires of the four of us in this collaboration. Ben's needs and preferences were equally important to acknowledge: yes to him continuing his gum chewing privilege, but not mint, and not in the car or in an enclosed space in which Cooper couldn't leave the environment. Steven, Ben, and I continued to brush our teeth with mint toothpaste. I continued to laugh anytime an opportunity presented itself—which became less frequent. Steven ate his bananas—but there was less singing in the house.

I continued practicing Ross Greene's CPS strategies and walking on eggshells around Cooper until the end of his sophomore year in high school. By then, we had collectively conquered physical safety issues and most emotional explosions. The lessons from Dr. Greene didn't transform our home into the Cleaver residence, but safety, some laughter, and sounds of music had returned.

CHAPTER 8

WHEN MADNESS NEXT
DESCENDS...DR. MICHAEL OKUN

> *Doubt ... is an illness that comes from*
> *knowledge and leads to madness.*
> —GUSTAV FLAUBERT

I n a war against mental illness, the ravages of battle—wounds that will never heal, struggles that leave you scarred—obscure victory. You become a lone soldier with indefatigable resolve to fight the next unpredictable trauma from a brain that will betray you, an invisible foe you must live with every moment of your life. Depression, OCD, Tourette's, and mood disorders are just a few diagnoses with symptoms that exhibit, diminish, and reappear without warning. You become haunted, hypnotized by a metered sound—*tick-tock, tick-tock, tick-tock*—as though a metronome were imbedded in your subconscious mind. *"It's just a matter of time until the next unexpected episode,"* you think to yourself. *"Not today,"* you pray.

Figuratively, mental illness is contagious in that it infects the entire family. After our son Ben was diagnosed with OCD and anxiety, and Cooper was diagnosed with Tourette's syndrome, OCD, ADD, and a mood disorder, we learned to adapt to every unexpected circumstance that required our attention. We'd learned to ignore the judgment and sneers from teachers, family members, and peers about how we disciplined our children. I simply didn't have the luxury to care what people thought about the decisions I made under circumstances they couldn't possibly understand.

In 2010, Ben was a high school junior, and Cooper was a freshman. After six years of our after-school activities consisting of dropping off or picking up prescriptions at pharmacies and driving to cognitive behavior therapy sessions, I finally began to understand that there are no cures, and there are no experts. Neuroscience had made aggressive advances, with claims that researchers had learned more about the brain in the last ten years than they had discovered in the previous century. Yet all of that new research wasn't enough to prevent the devastating compulsions of OCD, the paralyzing fears of anxiety, or the punishing, involuntary tics of Tourette's from reoccurring. Even with access to excellent medical care, I was still essentially on my own.

I, too, heard the clicks of the metronome chasing me, urging me forward. If I ever let my guard down the stress, exhaustion, and fear would seduce me, but I couldn't let myself give in. My sons counted on me. I had to learn more about their conditions to ensure the best treatment decisions, and I couldn't become overwhelmed by the constant disruptions of unexpected co-occurring symptoms that required new drugs. I learned that the only certainty was change.

We would always need more options when one drug stopped working, when one specialist needed to consult another, when one situation morphed into something else. Drummed into my brain were the pharmaceutical side effects that scared me the most, like tardive dyskinesia: a disorder resulting in involuntary facial grimacing, lip smacking or puckering, or involuntary tongue movements. This neurological disorder most frequently occurs as the result of long-term or high-dose use of antipsychotic drugs. Of course, practically every one of the drugs in our emporium included possible side effects of depression and suicide.

Early on, I asked simple questions about homeopathic therapies, vitamins, and nutrition. I read trade publications such as *Journal of the American Medical Association, New England Journal of Medicine,* and *Psychology Today*; and then I gradually progressed onto the NIMH website and reviewed some *PubMed* research studies.

One study touted electroconvulsive therapy (ECT), or shock therapy, which had re-emerged since the 1950s as a treatment for depression. Apparently, it was now less draconian, with minimally induced seizures and shock, and I was intrigued. In 2005, the U.S. Food and Drug Administration (FDA) approved Vagus nerve stimulation (VNS) for epilepsy and treatment-resistant depression. VNS works through a device implanted under the skin that sends electrical pulses through the left vagus nerve, half of a prominent pair of nerves that run from the brainstem through the neck and down to each side of the chest and abdomen. The vagus nerves carry messages from the brain to the body's major organs and to areas of the brain that control mood, sleep, and other functions. The pulses also appeared to alter certain neurotransmitters (brain chemicals) associated with mood. However, studies testing effectiveness of VNS in treating major depression are mixed.

Repeated Transcranial Magnetic Stimulation (rTMS) was a new technology that had gained FDA approval in 2008 for treatment-resistant depression and mood disorders. rTMS is a non-invasive treatment using a large electromagnetic coil placed against the scalp. The coil generates focused pulses that pass through the skull and stimulate the cerebral cortex, the brain's mood regulation domain. If it could help my sons, I had to know about it.

I read about several researchers around the world studying optogenetics, a technique that genetically modifies brain neurons and makes them light sensitive. Wavelengths of light can then be used to stimulate or reduce specific neuron activity. However, this treatment was too far down the road. The most recent research for mood and depression, with immediate results, and no impact on memory loss, was low-field magnetic stimulation (LFMS). Using LFMS, a patient is on a table, and his head slides into a capsule that looks similar to an MRI machine. The breakthrough with LFMS is that it has an immediate effect on mood— unlike ECT or TMS, which can take four to six week before results are noticed. LFMS uses magnetic fields that are a fraction of the strength, but are at a much higher frequency than electromagnetic fields with ECT or TMS.

In the fall of 2010, my cousin Andrew left me a message on the answer machine: "I just heard this neuroscientist at a lecture I attended on Parkinson's and movement disorders. I told him about the boys, and Dr. Okun is expecting your call." Excited, I jotted down the phone number, happy that my cousin was looking out for me. Andrew lived in Florida and served on the Psoriatic Arthritis Foundation Board, where he often learned about cutting-edge medical breakthroughs.

Dr. Michael Okun is co-director of the Center for Movement Disorders and Neurorestoration at the University of Florida College of Medicine. He's the National Medical Director for the Parkinson Foundation and runs the online international "Ask the Expert" forums on the National Parkinson Foundation website. His book, *Parkinson's Treatment: 10 Secrets to a Happier Life*, was a number-one best seller on Amazon. Having had a life-long career studying movement disorders, Okun was also a medical director for the Tourette Association of America.

Dr. Okun is a pioneer, and in 2010, he became one of a handful of specialists in the field of brain research and movement disorders that successfully performed Deep Brain Stimulation (DBS), a surgical procedure that involves implanting electrodes into select targets of the brain. These electrodes are used to interrupt faulty communication between brain regions that cause disabling, uncontrollable body movements.

I called Dr. Okun and reminded him that my cousin Andrew had referred me. I provided a brief history about Cooper's Tourette's and told him that Cooper had participated in the CBIT clinical trial for habit reversal at UCLA.

"The cognitive behavior intervention therapy was fairly successful—at least for a while," I told Dr. Okun. "If my son's tics worsen again, I need to know what more can be done to help him. Do you have time to briefly discuss DBS with me?"

"I'd be glad to," he said, speaking with patience and confidence in a slightly southern accent. "The work we're doing here is extremely promising, and we're seeing real success for patients with Parkinson's."

"What about for Tourette's?" I asked. "How invasive is it, and how does it work?"

Okun spent a generous amount of time on the phone with me, explaining the extraordinary precision of the surgery. First, a neurosurgeon injects anesthesia into the scalp and then uses a drill to create a dime-size hole in the skull where the microelectrode will be inserted. The team's neurologist then performs the microelectrode recording, which is visible on a monitor. The recording guides the neurosurgeon and neurologist in placing the electrode's lead in the exact area of the brain that will give optimal results. This part of the surgery can take several hours, depending upon the number of microelectrode passes needed to pin-point the target site. After the microelectrode recording has precisely located the target, the permanent DBS leads are placed inside the brain and connected to an implantable pulse generator, or IPG.

Dr. Okun was infectious in describing the promise of DBS. He informed me about successful surgeries that had been done to eliminate obsessional thoughts in OCD. "Yes," I agreed. "This is exciting new terrain." I was so desperate for treatment alternatives that I somehow managed to ignore the fact that he was describing a deeply invasive surgery into the brain, a procedure so outlandish that, just a few years prior, no one would have believed it could have been done. Instead, all I heard was that there would be no more trial-and-error drugs with intolerable side effects. The long-term benefits sounded encouraging, and this treatment was on the verge of becoming FDA-approved for Tourette's.

"If you're interested," Okun offered, "I'd be happy to meet with your sons the next time you're in Florida."

Of course I was interested, and imagined that we would one day go to Florida and meet Dr. Michael Okun and learn more about his program, and maybe—just maybe—his surgery could help. As I had done so many times before with so many drugs and doctors and procedures, I felt relieved, like I had finally found the holy grail of treatments. Dr. Okun followed up with an e-mail and contact information for a possible future consultation. My cousin was right—Dr. Michael Okun was a neuroscience rock star we needed to know.

I hung up the phone and a few minutes later thought—*Wait, am I crazy? Electrodes in the brain?* Yet, Okun's description of the surgery sounded uncomplicated, uncluttered, sort of like a heart defibrillator. Many lives are saved every day because of heart defibrillators.

Okay, I thought. *Brain-in-a-box.* I filed my notes from the call, and just as I was about to share this information with Steven, I found myself hesitant. *Whoa, slow down,* a voice inside reprimanded. It suddenly dawned on me that a brain is not a heart.

Was I seriously considering DBS? Steven had always been more cautious than I was, and anticipating his response to Dr. Okun's surgery made me think I'd gone crazy to consider it. There was *no* way he would ever allow anyone to drill a hole in his son's head! I could already picture him asking, and I hadn't even told him about how the wires and the leads hooked up to a small box that would transform our son into the Energizer Bunny.

But, hold on a minute—our brains are networks of electricity anyway, right? So DBS would make total sense, wouldn't it? Then I realized, IPGs run on batteries—what happens when the batteries wear out, or if they become defective? I hadn't thought about the long-term maintenance of DBS. These leads are implanted directly in the brain, so biocompatibility must be a concern. Crossing the blood-brain barrier could wreak havoc on the brain, because the brain's immune system acts differently from the body's immune system. I hadn't even considered asking Dr. Okun about dopamine pumps—or new therapies in development.

Despite this conversation I had with myself, I still wondered just what was I thinking, what made me so okay with this procedure as a possibility? How could I so effortlessly consider a surgery that would leave a permanent hole in my son's skull? And what about Cooper? He might despise me if I told him about this. He'd look at me with his round, trusting eyes, wondering how his mother, who supposedly loved and protected him, could possibly suggest drilling a hole into his cranium. Cooper's tics had given him a slight reprieve, and that's all he could embrace for the time being. He couldn't imagine planning for tomorrows, for the possibility of a return of tics so overpowering that DBS would feel like a welcome option. No, bringing this up now would only make it appear as though I were undermining his ability to control his body.

I was getting way ahead of myself because this wasn't elective surgery. Dr. Okun would first spend a good amount of time with us, and Cooper, before he would determine whether or not Cooper even met the criteria for DBS. I was so preoccupied with trying to remain hopeful and finding cutting-edge treatment options that I simply wasn't thinking clearly. Was drilling a hole in my kid's skull going too far? What was the defining line for quality of life within treatment options? At what point would my efforts to seek the best medical treatment outcomes for my family result in diminishing returns? Yes, Dr. Michael Okun was the rock star of DBS, and I was so grateful to learn about his profound successes and his burgeoning support from the Tourette Association of America. However, this wasn't the right time to further explore DBS. I continued this argument with myself until the dénouement, when the sinking sadness of reason returned. For now, DBS would be at the bottom of my list, just above hopeless.

CHAPTER 9

HELP ON THE WAY...
DR. ADAM GAZZALEY

The universe is not indifferent to our
existence—it depends on it.
—STEPHEN HAWKING

I gazed at the redwood tree outside my window, feeling vulnerable, bereft of vitality.

Caw! Caw! Caw! The chatter of those big black crows, squawking to each other on the tree branches, taunted me. They fluttered their massive, black wings, flapping them up and down and picking up speed until they were out of sight, moving on with fixed purpose.

I would not be left behind, I thought to myself. I, too, would keep moving. I, too, would have a charted course. I would have a plan for when madness next descended on our house.

My research quickly escalated to reading *PubMed* abstracts on the NIMH website, which provided links to a vast array of recent and historic studies. I was frenetic on my computer, clicking one hyperlink after another until I realized that I was becoming much too familiar with the CVs of the country's leading brain research scientists. Suddenly, terror struck, because I understood so little about what mattered most: identifying successful and sustainable mental health care for my sons.

I thought back to Dr. John Lilly and his early research implanting electrodes into the brains of dolphins and stimulating unique sensory responses. If his research in the 1960s hadn't been thwarted, DBS might be more commonplace today. In an average three-pound human brain, hundreds of thousands of chemical reactions occur every second. An average nerve cell forms approximately 1,000 synapses—the intercellular space between neurons—and it's been estimated that there are more synapses in the human brain than there are stars in our galaxy. Caltech neuroscientist and 1981 Nobel Laureate Roger Sperry's regeneration experiments revealed that there are chemotropic substances that are specific to each fiber. I understood how DBS was performed, but as a new surgery, scientists had little evidence about the long-term effects on the brain, the nervous system, and the body.

During this time, I was consulting for only one client and would get home early, before five. I was afraid to tell Steven about my late-night research project because I thought he'd think I was crazy and call it a waste of my time. While I knew it was a ridiculous obsession to read about clinical trials with statistics and math formulas I didn't understand, I still continued doing it. I read about new drugs and chemical compounds that, even with the aid of a dictionary and Google, I couldn't possibly digest. Undeterred, I remained stealth in my mission. Closing my office door I would feel like a spy, turning on my computer and focusing on one topic each night, whether it was drugs, clinical trials, newly touted research, or the various leading neuroscientists.

I spent many nights of many months of many years organizing my notes, just like the groupie who records every city, venue, date, opening act, and set list of her favorite rock band. The groupie always knows each band member's whereabouts, the girlfriend's and the wife's name until the groupie feels like she is embedded in her rock idol's life, too. I understood this frame of mind, because there were times when I imagined conversations or impressive e-mails where I'd pretended I had written to an esteemed Yale OCD researcher or clinician in Cambridge, and he'd be so blown away with my provocative query that he'd call me up himself!

Soon I began to go further than just reading, and joined several organizations. As a dues-paying member I could keep abreast of topical information. One such organization was Learning and the Brain, which sponsors events and symposiums for educators, social workers, psychiatrists, and neurologists. I'm sure I was one of very few lay members. Through L&B, I discovered Dr. Adam Gazzaley, founding director of the Neuroscience Imaging Center at the University of California San Francisco (UCSF), an associate professor in Neurology, Physiology, and Psychiatry, and the principal investigator of a renowned cognitive neuroscience laboratory.

In 2012, PBS sponsored The Distracted Mind, hosted by Dr. Adam Gazzaley. For the broadcast special, Gazzaley presented the scientific results of technology, information, social media, and messages that constantly vie for our attention, and how this affects our ability to focus. Most profoundly, the latest research suggests that multi-tasking is a myth. In the DVD release of The Distracted Mind, Gazzaley reveals the negative impact that multi-tasking has on our safety, memory, education, careers, and personal lives. It diminishes our attention because our brain cannot absorb, recall, or process this mega-data at such heightened demand. However, on a more positive note, Dr. Gazzaley explains what we can do to improve our attention. We can change our brains by changing our behavior.

After watching the documentary, I considered that perhaps we all have ADD; the collateral damage of our evolution. This culture of need for immediacy has changed and damaged our brain function. Maybe if Cooper lived in a different culture he wouldn't have ADD...or even if he did, no one would notice, or care. Do Aleut children, from the indigenous tribe of southwest Alaska, suffer from ADD, or OCD, or Tourette's? Regardless, Cooper's ADD diagnosis had been confirmed after he completed taking the Test of Variables of Attention (TOVA) diagnostic tool, a computerized, objective measure of attention and inhibitory control.

Months later I remembered, from working in the music business, that ex-Grateful Dead drummer, Mickey Hart, had been studying music and neurological issues for quite some time. He had served on the Board of The Institute for Music and Neurologic Function (IMNF), which is based in New York. The IMNF, co-founded by world-renowned neuroscientist Dr. Oliver Sacks, is considered to be the preeminent institute in clinical music therapy treatment, research, and education, using music to assist individuals with a wide range of neurological conditions including strokes, trauma, dementia, Alzheimer's, and Parkinson's diseases. Music therapy and the work at the IMNF was certainly something to consider. This was when I learned that Hart had been working with a renowned neuroscientist at UCSF. Hart and Dr. Adam Gazzaley were using drumming as a way to see the inside brain. The two had been working on identifying rhythms that can stimulate different parts of diseased and damaged brains.

Through recent research projects, including one funded by the GRAMMY Foundation's Grant Program, Dr. Gazzaley, along with a team of researchers, developed a groundbreaking brain rhythm therapy technology called *NeuroDrummer*, a custom-designed virtual reality rhythm training game directed at enhancing rhythmic abilities and helping people with neurological diseases. Another crazy coincidence for me was when, in 2014, I attended South by Southwest, an annual music industry convention in Austin, Texas. Dr. Gazzaley and Hart were scheduled to present a session, "Rhythm and the Brain."

Dr. Gazzaley began by explaining, "The question of how we fix brain rhythm disorders has puzzled neuroscientists for decades." Gazzaley and a team of UCSF scientists reported that they'd found a way to reverse negative effects of aging on the brain via a video game designed to improve cognitive control. *NeuroDrummer* was demoed by Hart during the session, giving attendees a firsthand look at the rapid response of brainwaves to sound and 3-D visuals. An earlier Magnetic Resonance Imaging (MRI) scan of Hart's brain, skull, and scalp tissue, as well as activity inside the brain recorded by signals measured at electrodes on his scalp, was displayed on a large screen. An electroencephalogram (EEG) is a test used to detect abnormalities related to electrical activity of the brain. This procedure tracks and records brain wave patterns. Small metal discs with thin wires (electrodes) are placed on the scalp, which then send signals to a computer to record the results. Hart was wearing an EEG cap. Through the use of very thin electrode wires, the EEG cap fabric enables simultaneous EEG recordings with TMS or fMRI. Each of the electrodes on Mickey's cap was detecting very subtle signals from rhythmic activity being generated by the neurons in his brain. After Hart began drumming, his brain waves were visualized, moving throughout his brain in real-time. It was awesome to see!

According to Mickey, "The only way to find the code on how music works is through science." He then explained, "Musicians and scientists know that the neural pathways are stimulated and reconnected when we play music or when people listen to music or are around music. Music is medicine, but it is also a legitimate brain therapy."

Rhythm is fundamental to how our brain organizes and understands information. There are multiple rhythms moving throughout the brain at different frequencies. Disruptions in this rhythm, also known as dysrhythmia, are associated with disorders such as depression, anxiety, schizophrenia, ADHD, and Tourette's syndrome.

Dr. Adam Gazzaley is a rock star in the field of neuro-electrics, using TMS, TES, fMRIs, and DBS in his studies to explore how we can enhance our cognitive abilities via engagement with custom-designed video games, and how using neurofeedback can reinforce adoption. He, too, had conducted numerous studies producing scientific evidence about the brain's plasticity and its ability to change. Gazzaley's lab intrigued me because his work supported Cooper's claims about the benefits of learning through gaming.

Project EVO, a videogame therapy for ADHD, is Dr. Gazzaley's most recent venture with Akili Interactive. This highly credentialed, respected, innovative neuroscientist was employing video games to enhance cognition during a time when each therapist Cooper saw warned Steven and me about the evils of the one domain in which Cooper thrived. Appropriate online gaming was an environment in which Cooper wasn't judged for having tics, and rule-based play expanded his self-esteem. This was around the time when Cooper's vocabulary flourished, and he'd proudly remark, "I learned that word from one of my games. See, gaming is educational for me." Or, he'd say, "It relaxes my tics when I game." On days when his tics subsided, he'd return to the piano and play an instrumental theme from a favorite video game. A therapy that combined music and gaming would certainly resonate with Cooper.

According to the website for The Gazzaley Lab at UCSF, Dr. Gazzaley also oversees the Neuroscape Lab, home to the 3-D Glass brain. This 3-D visualization allows one to see brain activity and connectivity in real-time. I remained on his website, thinking, *This is crazy, awesome!* Choirs of "Kyrie Eleison" and "Hallelujah" filled my head because there was now a viable way of looking inside the brain without drilling a hole into it. I decided that this was our next option, the place we would go if or when disaster next struck.

As soon as I realized such a safety net existed, the metronome stopped and no more panic-stricken moments would be stolen from my life. I wasn't looking for a cure, but for a reason to remain hopeful and strong. I needed to know that in the next worse moment we might face, things would somehow be okay, and if not, there was somewhere to turn. That somewhere was Dr. Adam Gazzaley.

Throughout my life, synchronicity would emerge like a beacon. And when it happened, I'd remember that I was connected to something greater than me, something good. Shortly after I added Dr. Gazzaley to my list of rock stars, I noticed that he would be speaking at a TEDMED event, which also featured a friend of mine. I sent her a text to congratulate her for this honor before begging her to introduce me to Dr. Gazzaley.

I've never called Dr. Gazzaley. I've never shaken his hand. But I know that he, and many other brilliant minds, share a steadfast commitment to end the suffering of those plagued by mental illness. It is in recognizing their extraordinary work and achievements that we can appreciate the good in humanity and understand how compassion and altruism connect us to each other. Hamlet was right when he spoke, "What a piece of work is a man! How noble in reason, how infinite in faculty! In form and moving how express and admirable!"

CHAPTER 10

CONSCIOUSNESS, BIAS, AND DRUGS...DR. ANDREW WEIL

*The psychic task which a person can and
must set for himself is not to feel secure,
but to be able to tolerate insecurity.*
—ERIC FROMM

Ben's hypochondria cycle began during his senior year in high school. The sudden appearance of something benign that most people would tolerate, such as a blister on his tongue, spiraled into a condition that he believed required immediate medical attention. I would say what any parent would.

"Rinse your mouth with diluted peroxide, and if it's not at all better by tomorrow, I'll call the doctor."

Of course, while we were all asleep, Ben was up half the night perusing the Internet, cherry-picking similar symptoms that could have catastrophic results, like mouth cancer. However, it wasn't until he insisted that I get him to the doctor for an AIDS test that his idiosyncrasies snow-balled into an avalanche that nearly destroyed us all.

After what appeared to be a typical day at school, Ben had a snack and went into his room to begin homework. A few minutes later, I heard his voice call out to me, sounding extremely troubled.

"Mom, where are you?" he called. "I need your help!"

He had something to tell me, but would only tell me in private, so I took him seriously as he closed his bedroom door. I sat on the floor in his room, and he was curled into his beanbag chair as he began his confessional.

"I'm so sorry, Mom," he said, pulling at his T-shirt collar. "I'm so sorry I never told you about a party I went to after school a few weeks ago."

"Ben, what are you talking about? What party?" I asked, thinking he might be on the brink of having a panic attack.

"Kids were drinking and there were drugs." Ben's voice cracked, and he began to wail. "I'm so afraid, Mom! I need to have an AIDS test, please," he pleaded.

"An AIDS test, for what?" This concern seemed to come out of thin air, but Ben looked terrified. "Whose party was it? When did you go to a party? Whom did you go with?" I had a hard time imagining someone as cautious and as fearful as Ben putting himself in such a compromising situation.

"Just these kids from school," he said with a response I found too dismissive. "You don't know them."

Ben described the scene; he remembered drinking some punch from a large bowl, then leaving his cup on a round table. He thought someone might have spiked his drink because he suddenly felt tired and had fallen asleep. All he remembered was seeing needles on the table before he nodded off. As soon as he awakened, he left and took the bus home.

"I think something happened to me at the party," he sobbed, as huge teardrops flowed down his cheeks. "I got woozy after I drank the punch and now I think I have AIDS."

I couldn't recall Ben ever coming home from school particularly disturbed, groggy, or angry, so I wasn't sure where such unbridled fear was coming from. "What does the drink have to do with AIDS?" I asked. "How do you think you were infected?"

He thought that someone stabbed him in between his toes with a used needle when he was asleep. The account was very detailed and his present trauma was deeply concerning, but something about this story didn't make sense to me.

"Ben, you're going to be okay," I said, "but I want you to explain what happened to Dad."

"You have to call the doctor," he said, becoming increasingly agitated. "I need an AIDS test! I don't want to die," he moaned, clutching his neck.

The problem with his story was that it changed, ever so slightly, when he repeated it for Steven, and that's when I discovered that the street name where he said this party took place didn't even exist in Santa Monica. I then remembered him telling me several weeks earlier about a girl in his class who was out sick most of the semester because she had AIDS. When I confronted Ben about this, suggesting that he was taking on this girl's story, he lashed out, accusing me of never believing him when he needed me most. He became hysterical, begging, pleading with us to get him tested for AIDS.

He continued going berserk until Steven said, "Look, if an AIDS test will calm him down, make an appointment for him in the morning." Although I knew we were enabling his OCD compulsion, I relented and picked up the phone to schedule the blood test. Ben was so out of control, so tortured, nothing would still his mind until he had that test.

After I left a message with the doctor's office to make the appointment, I confronted Ben about his fictitious narrative. "Why all the details about this party you didn't attend?" I asked softly. He finally admitted that he had made up the party story because it was the only way, he believed, we'd send him to the doctor for an AIDS test—and he was right. When the test came back negative, his obsessional fear was only temporarily mitigated. Over the years, there would be other useless AIDS tests, along with much graver circumstances in the not-too-distant future.

On August 10, 2013, I had fallen asleep by 10:00 p.m., because at 5:30 a.m. the next morning, a car would be taking Ben and me to LAX. We were flying to upstate New York, where Ben would be starting college as a freshman. Instead of sleeping peacefully, however, I was abruptly awakened by the sound of thumping up and down the stairs. Someone was stomping with increasingly purposeful punctuation, landing hard on each step. I opened my bedroom door and heard crying across the hall. It was Ben, except the crying escalated into guttural, tormented wails. Cooper was already in the bathroom, sitting on the floor beside him when Steven and I ran in, unable to comprehend why the four of us were in the bathroom at one in the morning. In four hours we'd be leaving to go to the airport—that was the plan.

Ben told us he had swallowed between six and eight Tylenol PMs; he tried to kill himself. He said he freaked out when he woke up and realized he was still alive. My memory of what happened next is fractured, like a crystal bowl smashed on a floor. The four of us became slivers of something past.

My eyes quickly inspected the scene for evidence and focused on the one empty pill casing in the bathroom trashcan. I also grabbed his "note," placed strategically on his desk, too noticeable to miss. I scanned what was written on the college-ruled paper and folded it in my hand to ensure that Steven and Cooper did not read it. Why add to their pain?

Steven began to yell, unable to fathom how someone he loved with all of his heart could betray him.

"Are you CRAZY? What were you thinking? YOU'RE NOT THINKING! WHAT HAPPENED TO YOUR BRAIN! WHY WOULD YOU RUIN YOUR LIFE? HOW COULD YOU GIVE THIS ALL UP? YOUR LIFE? COLLEGE? YOUR SCHOLARSHIP? WHAT HAVE YOU DONE, BEN?"

Steven looked almost translucent, colorless, like the blood had drained out of his body. He was incredulous that anyone would jeopardize a $160,000 scholarship and, essentially, his entire future. Watching my husband slump to the floor like a marionette, ashen and defeated, broke my heart. He adored Ben, and had been so proud of his academic success, his drive to achieve.

The loudest voice above this ongoing clamor was Ben's, screaming, "YOU DON'T GET IT! I DON'T KNOW WHAT I WANT TO DO WITH MY LIFE! I DON'T KNOW WHERE I WANT TO GO TO COLLEGE! I DON'T EVEN KNOW WHO I AM!"

We sustained his wild screams and tortured cries. The un-syncopated wails echoed throughout the bathroom, amplified sounds like otherworldly booms from overhead, until the gods, pathetic to our grief, moaned, "*You're really fucked now.*"

Yes, we really are, I thought listlessly.

Steven began to cry. I looked at our swollen, disfigured faces. How quickly beauty and intellect decay and putrefy one's soul. I looked at Ben, realizing that the son I thought I knew was gone, leaving behind this shell of his former self. I could not feel the love in my heart. I knew it had to be there, but somehow, it had been misplaced. I hoped that I would find it after the numbness disappeared.

We discussed next steps. I'd be on "Ben watch" until I could call our neurologist at seven thirty, in order to have Ben admitted into the Resnick NPI for a 72-hour watch. In the State of California, this is an involuntary psychiatric hold known as a 5150. I knew that Ben did not want to die. I knew that whatever he'd attempted to do would not have killed him, and believed he knew that, too. Nonetheless, the message came through loud and clear: our son needed help, and he needed it now. Cooper stayed with us downstairs, and by 4:00 a.m., he was not only exhausted, but he was also angry with Ben. As things began to connect in his mind, he gave his brother an ultimatum.

"We all have problems in our lives," he told Ben. "Either you choose to live and care enough to work yours out, as I have, or you don't. And if you choose number two, I will never forgive you."

Ben had always been the center of Cooper's universe. From the moment he was born, Cooper revered his older brother. Although the boys were opposites in demeanor, appearance, and interests, they were perhaps bound together because of their differences. They were each other's lifelong gift. Our friends couldn't believe it when they saw the boys together, sharing so much affection and acceptance. Sibling rivalry was too normal a problem to exist in our home, so theirs was a special relationship, for which I was always grateful. Now, I hurt for both of them, and tried to imagine life on the other side of this nightmare. Perhaps we'd reflect back on this as a night of forgiveness—for all of us.

Cooper went to bed. I remained in the den, either unwilling or unable to speak to Ben. I was consumed by dusty grayness; everything looked gray, sounded gray, smelled gray. Limp, lifeless gray like a gauze cloak, no texture, and no substance. Doing nothing while waiting for sunrise was the only thing more miserable than the situation itself. I took our college trip contact sheet from my luggage and began making cancellation calls.

With some teens, you always know what's going on with them because they tell you everything. Others, like Ben, are less emotive, less vocal, and seemingly less needy. I refer to these teens as "the silent killers," because you never really know what's going on inside their minds. Sitting on the couch, motionless and waiting for dawn, it struck me: these teens don't know, either. They don't know their own minds because they haven't developed insight, self-awareness, and consciousness.

Ben was a Teen Line listener at Cedars Sinai Hospital for three years in high school, had appeared in several school plays, and was featured in scientific news media citing a new learning module from his high school. He was more Google-able than my husband or me, and he not only actively engaged in life, but also seemed to genuinely enjoy participating in these activities, all of which he chose independently. My husband and I thought these successes reflected someone who knew his own mind, but apparently, he was a better actor than we had realized.

By ten on the morning after the scare, Ben was admitted to the Emergency Room at UCLA Hospital. The ER psychiatrist met with me after she examined him. "The team would like to admit Ben up to 96 hours, but certainly he could leave sooner," she said. "If he seems okay, we'd like him to go to college as planned and not lose his scholarship." I nodded in agreement. We were all on the same page.

Ben was placed in an observation room enclosed by glass walls, with a medical bed and a bathroom with a safety door that could not be locked. The security men posted outside the room had complete visual access. They told Ben that his knapsack had to remain with them.

A nurse walked me down the hallway to Ben's holding cell. I was astonished to see him on display in a big glass box, exposed, nowhere to hide. I thought about how awful it must have been for him, and how he looked like an animal in a cage with an audience waiting for him to do circus tricks. I kept telling myself that surely he would realize the benefit of dealing with his OCD and pushing on with his life. For two days he remained in the ER observation room with a book, *The Perks of Being a Wallflower*, placed like a prop on his bed. It was an interesting choice, bringing a story about "the world of first dates, family dramas, and new friends." This book selection did not escape the ER psychiatrist's intake notes.

After I got home, exhausted and empty, I kept focusing on Ben's pain and the layers of secrecy he had draped around his body like a shroud, so deeply veiled that I didn't see the depth of his anguish. I only saw deception and his previous unwillingness to acknowledge the extent to which OCD had interfered with his life.

"Why did he wait just four hours before we were supposed to fly out?" I wondered. Ben had all summer to tell us, or his therapist, or the school that he wasn't ready to go. Did he just now figure this out, or was he petrified of letting us down, of letting himself down? Ben had become terrorized by his own uncontrollable thoughts that contaminated his life. He had spun himself into a cocoon, so taut and fibrous that he couldn't get out.

Consciousness is the great human connector, because we all carry it around with us. Most of us spend our lives trying to understand our own consciousness on some level, and our conclusions determine how we choose to live. It is in knowing ourselves that we can know others, and this is what makes us human. Through consciousness, we develop empathy and compassion—which form our social connection. This reminds us that we are not alone, but part of something much greater than ourselves that is spiritually fulfilling. Without insight and consciousness Ben was alone, disconnected.

For me, some of the most profound observations about consciousness, bias, and drugs came from Dr. Andrew Weil in his book *The Natural Mind*. A Harvard-trained medical doctor whose botany thesis explored the narcotic properties of nutmeg, Weil eschewed the limitations and harmful effects of Western treatment in favor of a more integrated and effective approach to mental and physical health. After completing his residency at Massachusetts General Hospital and research for the National Institutes of Health (NIH), Weil spent more than twenty years studying and experiencing the recreational and medicinal effects of psychoactive drugs. His research revealed that certain plants produce chemicals that mimic the effects of substances made by the human brain. The medicinal benefits of certain plants—cannabis (marijuana leaves), psilocybin (mushrooms), mescaline (cactus peyote)—held, he believed, great promise for patients with treatment-resistant depression, severe pain, and alcoholism. Weil makes the point that the experiences people have when they take psychoactive drugs come from within, and that the alteration, or "high," comes from the nervous system, where the drug acts as a releaser.

Psychoactive is a term that is applied to drugs or other substances that change a person's mental state by affecting the way the brain and nervous system work. Frequently prescribed drugs used to treat conditions such as depression, anxiety, OCD, or ADHD include a palette of suppressants: SSRIs, anti-anxiety, and anti-pain drugs. Caffeine, nicotine, and alcohol were deemed the legal and socially acceptable choices to anesthetize pain, anxiety, and depression, and until only recently, addiction to these drugs or concern about their effects on our health and mortality went without scrutiny.

In 1994, Dr. Weil founded the Arizona Center for Integrative Medicine at the University of Arizona College of Medicine in Tucson, where he serves as its director and clinical professor of medicine and professor of public health. Weil is the author of many scientific and popular articles, including the international bestsellers *Spontaneous Healing,* and *Eight Weeks to Optimum Health.*

I've rarely shared my own feelings about psychoactive substances because the issues raised about drug use are profoundly emotional, personal, and biased. For many, the access to psychoactive drugs is the holy grail of our greatest hopes and fears. Yet, in order to understand the benefit of any drug, it's essential to understand how bias within the medical community, government regulatory agencies, and culture influence decisions about drugs and our access to them. However, according to Dr. Weil, "More powerful than drugs is the power of consciousness—its ability to heal the mind and, to some extent, the body."

Eighteen hours after he arrived at UCLA, Ben was finally placed in a private room at the NPI. The very least I expected was that someone would monitor him taking medication for depression or anxiety. According to Ben, Dr. Geary, his attending physician, didn't believe that he suffered from anxiety or OCD. Ben's nurse explained to Steven and me that per Ben's instructions, we weren't allowed access to his patient information. Ben was almost nineteen, and as an adult, HIPAA laws protected him.

When I questioned Ben about invoking HIPAA he denied it, but I did see a form in his room asking if his parents should be notified and he had placed a checkmark next to "no." Ben diffused this issue the same way he diffused other subjects, by speaking in vagaries and minimizing concerns. He was unclear about signing the forms, he explained, which was something he did the minute he was brought into his room. He was "very confused," at the time, and really didn't know what he was signing.

On Wednesday morning, I received a call from the NPI's social worker; she indicated that Ben would be discharged on Friday, August 16. Ben had already spent a combined five days in UCLA since we'd brought him to the Emergency Room. I went to visit him on Wednesday evening, during visiting hours. He was in his room, agitated and pacing, ranting rather than speaking to me.

"Have you slept?" I asked, taking in his sickly appearance. He looked much worse than he had five days earlier, much more exhausted. I surmised that he had lost 10 pounds.

"I want to leave here, Mom. I can't eat the food here. They don't even think I have OCD."

Against my better judgment, I ignored this piece of information. "Well, I have good news," I told him. "You're out of here Friday!"

"Mom, I don't think you can get me out of here."

"I just told you, the social worker said they plan to discharge you on Fri—"

"Mom, I'm telling you, you can't get me out. Dr. Geary told me there's going to be a hearing, and if I tried to challenge him, I would lose. You don't get it; you can't get me out!"

I stared at him. His demeanor displayed total resignation.

"I'm confused, Ben. The social worker told me you were being discharged. Is there something you're not explaining to me?"

"No, Mom. I just know that what they're telling you isn't what they're telling me."

I went to the nurses' station to have them page Dr. Geary. Fifteen minutes later, a resident appeared.

"Doctor, I don't understand what's going on here," I began. "What's Ben's treatment plan?"

First looking to Ben for approval, the resident then responded, "We don't see any indication of OCD—" but I wouldn't let him continue.

"You don't think he has OCD? You don't think he's depressed? He's in a lockdown facility!" I ranted. "I'm not sure who's crazy here! Please have Dr. Geary paged."

The resident wrote notes from our brief chat. "I'll leave a message for Dr. Geary to call you."

"Don't worry, Ben, we'll get you out of here," I assured him. "I'll call you tomorrow, after I've had a chance to speak with Geary."

Dr. Geary never returned my calls or e-mails. Fortunately, Dr. Erik, our neurologist who had helped with Ben's admission into the Resnick

NPI, phoned to see how we were holding up. He asked how Ben was doing now that he was placed on a fourteen-day hold. Unsure of what he
was talking about, I asked for clarification.

California law states that within the first seventy-two-hour hold, a
5250 must be written to continue the involuntary confinement of a patient for another fourteen days, and apparently, this had already been
done without our knowledge. There had been a hearing, which Geary
mentioned to Ben, in advance; but neither Steven nor I knew anything
about it. The result of this hearing, by California State Court order, meant
that Ben wasn't leaving UCLA on Friday after all.

Later, I would learn that after I left Ben on that first day in his hospital room, several physicians went in and performed a detailed evaluation, asking him a number of questions. Unfortunately, his response to
one of those questions was: "I don't want to wake up." When I heard this,
I couldn't believe it. I couldn't understand why he would have said something remotely close to death ideation to a resident in the psych ward. I
knew he didn't mean it, not deep down, and I found myself wondering
if he was just testing them. After I accepted my complete powerlessness,
I realized that the one benefit of Ben staying in the hospital was that he
would be medicated. I didn't want him home if he couldn't be rational.
His only coping mechanism, the narratives he had been telling himself
and all the rest of us, were too destructive.

Still, I couldn't fathom how a legal proceeding in a psych ward involving a mentally distressed nineteen-year-old kid who was 100 percent financially dependent on his parents could occur without parental
consent or knowledge. I brought Ben into UCLA for a seventy-two-hour
watch, which turned into a fourteen-day involuntary hold, determined
by Dr. Geary and the State of California. You do not get to pick your
attending in a psych ward—it's luck of the draw. Dr. Geary refused to
have a phone conversation with either Ben's therapist, who had treated

Ben's OCD for more than four years, or me. Instead, Dr. Geary gave our son a new diagnosis of Borderline Personality Disorder (BPD). The cognitive therapy for OCD versus BPD is very different, according to the two psychiatrists with whom I consulted. They both believed that Geary's diagnosis and the treatment for BPD would do Ben more harm than good.

Ben needed help, but he also needed to get out of UCLA. The only person providing my husband and me with snippets of information was the hospital social worker, who only contributed additional stress and confusion to the situation. My son became inaccessible to me, and I wanted him back. I wanted to get him the help he needed.

Ben was finally discharged from the NPI on August 23. However, Dr. Geary's release orders stated that he would not approve outpatient OCD therapy as an option because Ben required intense therapy. I had already called the OCD Institute at McLean Hospital in Massachusetts—which was the mutually agreed upon treatment program for Ben.

Steven and I made our feelings known, too. Ben's discharge home would be conditional and temporary—until he was accepted into McLean. Ben would attend weekly therapy appointments and take his medication, which Steven or I would oversee, every morning. He would not be allowed to lock his bedroom door.

After the Labor Day holiday weekend, I again followed up with Admissions at the OCD Institute at McLean Hospital. The program's director, Diane Davey, answered the phone, and confirmed that Ben had met the diagnostic criteria for acceptance into the program. However, to ensure his ability to actively engage in their rigorous treatment plan, he had to be stable before entering their facility. Unlike at UCLA, McLean would not have a suicide watch over him. Diane made it clear that Ben had to want to be there. I assured her that we accepted the expectations of the program. McLean was the best and only option, and Ben had to get better. He *would* get better.

I hung up after talking to Diane feeling hopeful that we had a plan, but anxious about the wait. Ben couldn't go to McLean until a spot at the facility became available and we had no idea when one of the 20 beds would become vacant. Diane asked me to check in with her in a few weeks, and every minute of every day within those few weeks stole chunks of my heart and our family's lives. Nothing positive would happen until Ben was there—no miracles would occur in our home. Finally, on September 28, we got the call for Ben to come to McLean, and I booked two one-way flights to Boston.

"You have to make a genuine effort in the program, because they'll kick you out if you don't want to get better. Too many other kids on that 5-month-long waiting list are willing to work hard," Steven told Ben.

"I promise you that I'll try," Ben said, "but I can't promise you that I'll stay eight weeks. I promise to try and work the program for *two* weeks instead."

None of us knew what Ben would be facing, and in reality, we knew he wasn't in a position to make any promises. McLean was the place, the opportunity for Ben to acknowledge and learn how to manage his OCD and anxiety. Ben didn't want to die, and now he knew that in choosing to live, there would be no shortcuts, no CliffsNotes.

The residential OCD program typically ranged from 3 to 8 weeks; I packed suitcases with all-weather clothing for both of us. Neither Steven nor I could understand how our lives had come to this point, how we were flying Ben to a hospital in Boston instead of flying him to college in New York. We felt physically beaten by an unknown force, but we knew it was the right decision. Our love for Ben was far greater than our pain. Ever the optimist, I believed that as long as there was a treatment opportunity, there was hope.

Finally on our way to Boston, Ben and I made our way through the American Airlines terminal and headed to our gate. Pulling my carry on with one hand, holding my purse and our boarding passes with the other, I couldn't believe my eyes. Being far-sighted, I was shocked to spot Dr. Andrew Weil walking in our direction. I would have recognized him anywhere, that great, burly man with the beard and balding head. I moved towards him as though a magnetic force had practically pushed me right in front of him. I stopped and waited until our eyes met. Saddled with the weight of the events of the last several months, the strings pulling at my sad heart left me tangled up in anguish and distraction. I wanted to shake his hand, since greeting a stranger with a handshake seemed a more intimate gesture, but I couldn't.

"Excuse me," I stuttered, feeling my heart race with the excitement of an unofficial member of the Dr. Andrew Weil fan club. I was so terribly nervous that a bizarre sequence of words bolted out of my mouth. "Hi, Dr. Weil. I loved…love…your work…your book, *The Natural Mind.*"

"Well, thank you," he said with a smile. His eyes twinkled with a particular warmth and serenity.

I felt my lips contort into a strangely placed grin. He asked me my name and I replied, "Faithe." No last name, no context about why I so blatantly made my presence known to him… just "Faithe."

"Well, very nice to meet you, Faithe."

After several awkward seconds of silence, we continued walking to our respective destinations. Deep down inside, I felt that Ben and I were part of this big universe, one in which we both belonged. My synchronistic moment with Dr. Weil was reinforcing; it was my affirmation that Ben was on his way to where he needed to be.

CHAPTER 11

McLean, Misery, and OCD...
Dr. Michael Jenike

> *Anxiety is love's greatest killer. It creates the failures.*
> *It makes others feel as you might when a drowning*
> *man holds onto you. You want to save him, but*
> *you know he will strangle you with his panic.*
> —Anais Nin

B en and I landed at Boston's Logan International Airport and checked into a hotel. The next morning, suitcases in our rental car, we followed the directions to a long, private drive in Belmont, Massachusetts. The arrow signs led us all the way to the top of the hill, and we had arrived at our destination: McLean Hospital, formerly known as the Asylum for the Insane. Our appointment with admissions was at nine. We were right on time.

"The campus is beautiful," I said, getting out of the car, admiring the voluptuous maple and oak trees; a reminder that the foliage would soon begin.

Although Ben didn't respond, I continued to marvel at the property, which was surrounded by acres of green hills and lush landscape. Several old buildings spread out across the front of the site in a U-shape, and at the back stood a large, nineteenth-century brick building covered in ivy. Founded in 1811, the name was changed to The McLean Asylum for the Insane in honor of its greatest benefactor, John McLean. In 1885, the McLean Asylum moved from its original site in Somerville, Massachusetts, to its current location in Belmont, approximately nine miles from Boston. Known for the famous people who have been treated there, McLean alums include Nobel Prize winner John Forbes Nash, whose life story was featured in the film *A Beautiful Mind*; singer-songwriter James Taylor; Pulitzer Prize-winning poet and Harvard instructor Robert Lowell; and Sylvia Plath, whose novel *The Bell Jar* reveals her disturbing spiral into depression, attempted suicides, and her experiences at a state psychiatric institution before moving to the posh and private McLean Hospital.

More than fifty years later, McLean had continued to maintain the world's largest neuroscientific and psychiatric research program within a private hospital. McLean is supported with resources from both Harvard Medical School and Massachusetts General Hospital. Dr. Michael Jenike is the founder of the Obsessive Compulsive Disorders Clinic and Research Unit at Massachusetts General Hospital, a professor of psychiatry at Harvard Medical School, and founder and director of the OCD Institute at McLean Hospital. Opened in 1997, the OCD Institute, or OCDI, became the country's first residential treatment program for individuals with OCD. Patients are admitted from all over the world to the twenty-bed residential program.

I had known about Dr. Jenike long before our arrival at McLean. I'll confess, there was once a time when I didn't know that the correct way to hang a roll of toilet paper was with the squares closest to you, not against the wall. Nor had it ever occurred to me that one must always use the third cup cover when getting a Slurpee at 7-Eleven. The hand-groping germs of others eliminate using the top cup cover and most people, of course, know that the second cup cover is also contaminated. I had been surrounded by OCD for more than two decades, and colliding into Michael Jenike was inevitable. It wasn't a matter of *if*, but where or when.

After checking into Admissions, Ben and I found our way to North Belknap to meet Diane. She wasn't available, but her assistant, James, met us, and brought Ben's suitcase to his dorm room and introduced him to his roommate. Ben would be Jeff's third roommate since he'd arrived at McLean three weeks earlier. Within moments of our stepping into the building, a bunch of older teens swarmed around Ben, the new kid. After giving me a modest hug, Ben waved for me to leave, and the kids rushed him into his orientation.

"Ben!" I called out. "I think we're supposed to meet with your social worker. Don't we need to go upstairs?"

"No, I'll do it later!" he called back. "I'm scheduled to meet with my therapist." He looked at me with a relenting nod and disappeared down the narrow hallway.

I stared at the warped wood floors in the small, funky residence hall, the golden retriever relaxing on the floor, and almost got caught up in a feeling that this was sort of cool. It was easy to forget that we were in a residential psychiatric institution whose mission was rigorous behavior modification. My son was supposed to be in college. There was little about this that was cool.

I walked towards the entrance, looking for Diane; she was waiting for me, and welcomed me into her office. After such a hectic morning, I found her warm demeanor comforting. She closed the door and we began reviewing Ben's schedule at the OCDI.

"We use a team approach," Diane said, "and each patient in the program is assigned a behavior therapist, a psychiatrist, and a family therapist or case manager, who are all in regular consultation with each other. Did you meet Terry?"

"No," I explained. "There seemed to be a conflict and Ben was scheduled for therapy."

Diane seemed confused. "That's too bad. I'll make sure Terry gets in touch with you before the end of the day." She scanned some notes and then asked, "When do you plan to return to Los Angeles?

"Not until after I've met with Terry and I've had a chance to discuss Ben's assessment and treatment." I reminded her that I'd be staying at my father's house, 35 minutes away. "I'm familiar with Dr. Jenike's success with treatment-resistant OCD patients, and we place our trust in him and the McLean OCDI program. This is Ben's best chance for conquering his OCD."

Diane smiled. "We'll do everything we can."

I tried to conceal my grave concern, the possibility that Ben wouldn't become another Jenike success story. Dr. Jenike is perhaps best known for his extraordinary work with Ed Zine, a young college athlete who exhibited the most severe case of OCD on record, which included, among other things, counting rituals that required 16,384 precise movements between getting from his bed to the bathroom every morning. Zine's story is chronicled in the book *Life in Rewind: The Story of a Young Courageous Man Who Persevered Over OCD and the Harvard Doctor Who Broke All the Rules to Help Him.* Helping Ben, by comparison, should have been a piece of cake—or so I hoped.

Dr. Michael Jenike was my rock star for helping patients with OCD, and he had been on my radar for years. Growing up in Boston, I had seen and heard Dr. Jenike interviewed on television and radio shows. Jenike is highly respected amongst his peers as an authority on treatment for

OCD and co-morbidities, and his empathy for those suffering from it is profound. Jenike was among the earliest OCD researchers and he pioneered treatments for the disorder. Since the 1970s, hundreds of doctors across the country now work with OCD patients. I trusted Dr. Jenike long before I met him, and felt so hopeful knowing that Ben was in his care.

"Everyone has intrusive thoughts, but in OCD, the distress is amazing," Jenike once explained during an NPR radio interview. "We see fairly sane people tormented by repetitive thoughts and ritualistic behavior that control their lives. There's a disconnect between what they know and what they feel, which causes immense suffering." He continued by explaining, "OCD is deeply rooted in anxiety. Performing compulsive rituals only temporarily relieves anxiety, resulting in a need to re-enact them again and again. The rituals consume an inordinate amount of time, making it impossible to meet the demands of a normal life."

After thanking Diane for her time and then parting ways, I walked across the campus back to the parking lot and stood in the bright sunlight. I was barely able to reconcile that I was moments away from leaving Ben not at college, but at a psychiatric institution. I cried in the car, grief-stricken over how terrible it was for my son to have to go through this and how powerless I felt in the face of his illness.

I decided to drive the country roads to my father's house in Southborough, with my newfound confidence gained from using the navigation system on my iPhone. Trees along both sides of the road were bursting with leaves ready to change color as sunlight danced through openings in the branches, guiding me home.

At the age of 83, my dad still had a full head of hair, though completely white. His boyhood face remained mostly unchanged, except for his jowls, which made him resemble an aged Paul McCartney, and his laugh was still as robust as ever. Like McCartney, my grandfather had been born in Liverpool, England; so I had always figured my dad's jowls were a British trait. After I hugged my father, I unpacked my things and fell asleep. I was exhausted, and didn't wake up until 5:00 p.m. I checked my phone, but Terry hadn't contacted me. If she didn't call by tomorrow and before the long holiday weekend, I'd have to endure five days without any status update about Ben.

On Thursday, rather than wait for Terry's call, I rallied my father and brother and proclaimed the day as an *"apple shmatzing"* day, which meant going to the apple orchards and gorging on freshly picked, lip-smacking good apples. *"Shmatzing"* (from our family lexicon) is the sound made from the first big crunch into the apple and sucking in the juice as it drips from your mouth. The Macoun apple (pronounced *Ma-cown* or *Ma-coon*) is my favorite fruit, and one of my favorite foods. The skin is dark, like a McIntosh, but with a purplish flush. Inside, the flawless, snow-white flesh is firm, crisp, and succulent, with a subtle taste of berry. Macouns are a rare delight, as the crop is only available from October to November. The stems of Macouns are very short, which forces the apple to push itself off the branch as the fruit matures. They must be picked at this precise time and before they can bruise or rot on the ground, which creates a very small window of opportunity to experience this Northeast treasure. We enjoyed our day of apple picking, but by late afternoon, I still hadn't heard from Terry.

It wasn't until Saturday afternoon when Ben called. Although I maintained my guard, I was terribly excited to hear his voice, and hear how he was doing.

"Mom, I hate it here," he whispered.

"I understand, but it's not supposed to feel like a vacation," I gently reminded him.

He'd only been there four days. Keeping him there four weeks would be a challenge.

"Did you have a checkup or any blood work drawn?" I asked.

He didn't say anything for a few seconds. He was filtering the topics for discussion, and I could tell that medication wasn't one of them. During the past year, Ben had either nothing to say, or he'd inject a conversation with unkind rancor.

"The food here is awful. I hardly eat." Ben explained that there were twelve people who ate together in his dining hall. "One guy ate four yoghurts, and they only brought us twelve, so a bunch of us didn't get any. Can you take me out to dinner tonight?"

This rapid fire of truncated factoids made me uneasy. Ben tended to accelerate conversations almost on purpose, as if he didn't really want me to understand. Over the last several years he had bamboozled me with this tactic, leaving me with the feeling that we had had a conversation about something, but without any specifics or details to remember in retrospect. Again, this time, he got to me. I was surprised that he wanted to see me, wanted to spend time with me. I was anxious to see how he looked.

"Is that okay, for us to have dinner together?" I asked. "What are the rules? I haven't even spoken to Terry yet."

"I just have to sign out with one of the counselors before I leave. I already told her that you were taking me out to dinner."

Ben had concocted this plan without knowing that I would be available, or even willing to come pick him up. Something didn't feel right to me, but I was so flummoxed by not knowing what was going on at McLean that I went along with the plan.

"Fine," I said. "I'll be there by six."

"Can you get here by five thirty? Meet me in the front, near the parking lot. Don't park in the back. Okay? At five thirty." These specific instructions were nothing new to me. I had become used to his subterfuge.

I didn't tell anyone that I was afraid of Ben or what he might do. His behavior had become completely unpredictable these past months, and

I wasn't comfortable taking him off campus. He was physically stronger than me. What would I do if he refused to get back in the car and I was out alone with him in the middle of nowhere?

I drove up the long road and into the parking lot on the top of the hill. Through flickering pink pastels and gold vermillion leaves hanging from the branches, I saw someone dressed in a dark olive sweatshirt approaching the car. Ben opened the door and got inside.

"Where are we going?" he asked.

"I brought a picnic dinner," I said. "Since the weather is so beautiful, I thought it might be nice to eat outside."

"You said we'd go out to eat."

His voice had a tone that sounded like an ungrateful accusation. It made me wish that I hadn't come to see him.

"Come on," I said. "Get out of the car. I brought sandwiches, chips, drinks, and apple toddies. I have some Macouns for you."

"We can't go out yet." Ben, still in the car, slid his body below the dashboard.

I felt a dart near my throat. Something *was* off, and I then knew for certain that I *had* been bamboozled. "What's going on, Ben?"

"They're going bowling tonight. You know I hate bowling. I told them I had dinner plans with you. If they see we haven't left, they might still try to make me go with them."

"Maybe being social and participating in social activities is part of your therapy."

"I'm with the same people all day, every day," he said as he curled his body into the shape of a roly-poly bug, on the floor of the front seat in the car. "It's okay."

I agreed to stay in the car, but I knew that people don't hide when things are okay. "*It's okay*" was Ben's usual justification for disassociating from the others.

We watched as four young adults emerged from a grassy area behind a building, laughing as they headed down the long road. Once they were out of sight, I took a large shopping bag out of the car and pointed to a picnic table.

"Let's sit over there," I suggested.

Ben sluggishly followed me to the table. "You said you'd take me out to eat. Why can't we go to a restaurant?" OCD can take control like a broken record, unable to move on to the next track.

"Look," I began, "you asked me to have dinner with you at the last minute. I don't know if I'm even allowed to take you anywhere."

"I can leave here anytime I want, you know. Being here is voluntary," he threatened.

I almost cried, thinking about all the previous therapists he'd never opened up to over the years; so much denial and wasted time. As hard as it was, I held back my tears.

"Being here is involuntary for you," I said. "This was your only ticket out of Resnick NPI."

"You couldn't have me committed," he said, likely thinking that I couldn't because he was over the age of eighteen.

"Actually, I could, and I would," I said, the timbre of my voice uncharacteristically deep. We were both quiet for a minute. "Don't you get it?" I implored. "There's nothing I wouldn't do to try to help you, Ben."

He looked away from me and picked up his ham and cheese sandwich. I almost reached out to touch his arm, but instead I looked down and tried to concentrate on something mundane to fight back my tears. I studied the second hand on my watch and noticed that each movement, from one number to the next, wasn't precisely the same. Intermittently, there was an imperceptible delay, almost as if the hand got stuck for a millisecond before it could catch up.

On the outside, Ben looked handsome and healthy. It was easy to forget that he was very sick—otherwise, he wouldn't have met the strict admission criteria for McLean. Inside, he was miserable, and his anguish became an infection that spread to his heart and mind. He couldn't even acknowledge my unconditional love for him. I would have given up anything to have our special mother-son moments back again. To hear his infectious laugh, to see his eyes light up, or to feel the touch of his small, soft hands holding my cheeks, I would have done anything. I would have swapped places with the devil to experience one more go at Rock, Paper, Scissors, the game we could never really play together because we always chose the same object. We were connected then. I knew who he was and how he felt; and if he needed me, I could help him. Now I wasn't so sure.

After a short walk, Ben wanted to go back to his room. I hugged him and said good-bye, glad to have seen him, glad to leave. I was exhausted from being with him.

Monday morning my phone rang, and to my relief, it was Terry, at long last. We set up an appointment to meet at three the following day. She said she would inform Ben about the meeting, and also suggested that we conference Steven in by phone. I told her that I had seen Ben on Saturday night and explained my concerns about him not taking his medication. Terry assured me that we'd address these issues together at tomorrow's session, but I was confused. It had been five days since Ben had arrived; why hadn't anyone addressed his medication?

The next day, I pulled into the parking lot at McLean about fifteen minutes before our meeting. I had just parked when Ben called my cell phone.

"Listen," he said. "If you get a call from Terry for a meeting today, don't come here. Okay?"

"Why not?"

"You don't need to be there," Ben insisted. "It's not a big deal. Just don't come. Promise me you won't."

"Good-bye, Ben." I hung up on him. I was finished with his twisted agendas, his panicked, last-minute attempts to control a situation, to control me with banishments that further eroded our relationship. Ben had become enslaved by his lies, and he was guarding his demons like a true foot soldier.

I crossed the parking lot, walked into the building, and waited upstairs outside Terry's office. Moments later, Ben turned down the hallway. "Why are you here?" he bellowed. "I TOLD YOU NOT TO COME!"

Terry opened the door to her office and invited us both in. Before either she or I had a chance to speak, Ben faced Terry and shouted, "YOU CANNOT SAY ANYTHING TO HER!" He stomped his foot on the floor like Rumpelstiltskin. He couldn't have me exiled from the meeting, and that just sent him reeling. Terry placed her hands gently on his shoulders and guided him into her room. The slight smile on her face told me that Ben's behavior was an all too familiar experience in family therapy. She began the session by explaining to us both that weekly family therapy was part of the OCDI program at McLean.

"Fine, then I won't talk," Ben said spitefully.

Terry was middle-aged and laid-back. Her shoulder-length hair was brown, in the process of graying, and her outdated glasses and lack of makeup accentuated her hackneyed style. *Who needs to look glamorous, working in a mental institution?* I realized.

"What don't you want me to discuss with your mother in front of you?" Terry asked.

She tried to understand Ben's concern, gently reassuring him that this was a time for the family to talk together, but he refused to participate. After sitting in silence for a while, Terry finally moved on and asked for Steven's number.

"NO!" Ben hollered. "I don't want him on the phone! It's too much for me! Don't you see I can't handle this?"

I was stunned. I couldn't understand why he was flipping out, but it was good for him to do it in front of Terry. Surely she would agree that Ben was irrational and that he needed to take his meds. As Terry called Steven, Ben began pacing around the worn velour couch until Terry asked him to sit and face her. By now, Steven was already on speakerphone.

"Hello?" Steven asked. "Boozie, are you there?"

I was so glad for Steven to be part of this session. I needed his support, but unfortunately, he didn't get a chance to hear my response.

Ben faced Terry, continuing to gabble nonsense. "This is impossible. It's too much for me. I can't talk to you with my mother here and with *him* on the phone! He talks over everyone and it stresses me out. I can't understand—"

Steven asked, "What's going on there?" But no one responded.

I glanced out the office's small, grimy window overlooking the back parking area, and again, with stunning clarity, I remembered that we were in a mental hospital. Ben continued his tantrum, rebuking Steven's genetics for giving him his problems, before turning his vehemence towards me.

"She's always moody. She thinks she's always right, but she never gets anything right!" Ben hammered.

I looked at Terry, wondering when she would take control of this frenzy, but she remained completely calm during Ben's conniption. The debate about Steven's participation in the session raged on until finally he volunteered to hang up and said good-bye, and still Terry only listened to Ben, carefully observing his behavior. *Good grief*, I thought at first. *Here's another therapist that Ben will find a way to manipulate.* Terry had remained still throughout Ben's tirade, but when she finally spoke, she exhibited a quiet confidence in dealing with him. I watched her lean in closer to connect with him, her voice even, but firm.

"This is what you need to work on, Ben. You have to learn that you can't control every situation in life. Just now, for example, with your dad, you wouldn't stop talking until you made him hang up the phone." She was spot on.

Terry asked him how his therapy was coming along. He responded by insisting that he wasn't like the other OCDers, and that his body dismorphic disorder (BDD) was different from his roommate's. His embarrassment about his body, he believed, was based on physical reality—unlike his roommate's concerns, which were exaggerated beliefs about his large nose, or his unibrow, which resulted in him spending a good amount of time in front the mirror applying makeup. Ben didn't like that the bathrooms at the OCDI were kept locked or that access had to be granted by staff. He hated having to ask for portions of hand soap and toilet paper, but there was a reason why quantities of these products were monitored for patient use.

At home, Ben never acknowledged his extraordinarily long showers, which were a waste of water and a significant cost on our monthly utility bill. The daily disappearances of full rolls of paper towels or toilet paper became a mysterious illusion, about which he always feigned innocence. Although it must have felt demeaning to have someone monitor his use of bathroom products, Ben needed to confront this common, yet problematic OCD washing ritual.

I interjected, "Terry, Ben told me he isn't on medication for anxiety or depression. Is that possible?"

Terry hadn't spoken to his doctor, who was out of town. I was incredulous, but she moved on to discuss Ben learning to treat Steven and me with more respect, and soon our first family therapy session was over. Terry confirmed that we'd meet the same time next week. I was too angry and sad to say anything to Ben. We went downstairs and walked outside at the same time, but we never said good-bye.

Ben's OCD triggered depression. Many symptoms of depression are private experiences, such as feeling an internal sense of loss, hopelessness, or sadness. As these feelings are all somewhat easy to conceal, Ben had fairly successfully hidden his depression from us, and his withdrawal from those he loved only reinforced his sense of loss. Depression is like a thief in the night, tiptoeing in silence, wearing an invisible cloak as it steals your heart, your life, and your soul.

I e-mailed Dr. Jenike, one of the two prescribing doctors at the OCDI. I asked for his advisement regarding the pharmacological aspect of Ben's treatment. It wasn't long before Jenike replied to my message. He believed Ben had an excellent and highly qualified treatment team, and that he needed to get on board with the program. Jenike was encouraging and felt things would be okay, as long as Ben followed his plan. I didn't want to further provoke this man, a brilliant OCD specialist and highly decorated US Navy officer, so I decided to back off. After all, Ben had counselors and therapists with him twelve hours a day, seven days a week. I had to remind myself that he wasn't in a temporary holding cell like he had been at Resnick. His acceptance into McLean had been extremely selective. Here, his treatment needs were all too familiar to someone as experienced with OCD as Dr. Jenike and the rest of his team.

Unfortunately, I didn't find McLean family therapy to be at all productive, and I dreaded returning only to be berated by my nineteen-year-old son. Our session on October 24, however, began on a much-improved note. Ben still seemed agitated, but he was coherent. I learned that his therapy included reflecting about friends he had abandoned and experiences he'd missed out on as a result of the interference of his OCD and BDD. For example, he was encouraged to go online, look up his former friends on Facebook, and see how they had moved on with their lives. As further part of this treatment, he had visited a friend from high school earlier in the week, who was now attending a nearby university.

Tears filled my eyes as I listened to Ben recount these memories. Terry asked me why I was crying.

"It's sad," I replied. "How is this therapeutic?"

"It's different from the typical exposure and response therapy," Ben explained. "I do it for about forty-five minutes. After I'm done, as a reward, I get to take my walks."

"Where do you go?" While it surprised me that Ben, who hadn't previously been an avid walker, now suddenly relished this activity, I remembered him hinting at it during our picnic dinner.

"Different places," he said. "Usually, I walk in the tunnels and listen to music on my iPhone."

I knew about the McLean tunnels, which were constructed in the late 1800s as an underground passageway connecting the private cottages and main buildings to the entire property. What I didn't know, at the time, was the benefit of the "see what you missed out on" therapy.

I later learned that Nate, Ben's behavior therapist, combined Acceptance and Commitment Therapy (ACT) to enhance Exposure and Response Therapy (ERT). ACT differs from traditional behavioral therapy in that, rather than trying to teach people to better control their thoughts, sensations, and memories, ACT teaches them to just notice and recognize the myriad of thoughts, especially the previously unwanted ones that stick in our heads like an uninvited guest. The goal is to move from cognitive fusion, to cognitive diffusion, to disentangle our web of preconceived good or bad narratives. The process is meant to increase psychological flexibility, awareness without judgment. Through this practice, an individual learns to identify personal values and to act on them, which results in bringing more meaning to life.

"I've been doing everything they tell me to do," Ben announced. "So, I'm ready to leave."

Terry rolled her chair closer to Ben. "You've only been here two weeks," she told him. "Your therapist thinks you should stay, and that you can benefit more by being here." I was relieved to hear Terry set him straight.

"I have to go home to do my college applications," Ben said.

"You know you can work on that here, Ben," Terry confirmed.

"No," he insisted. "I need to be home to do them."

Terry maintained her composure during this back and forth with Ben. "We have computers, phones, and all the resources you need here."

This was the first time Ben had mentioned college or any future plans. While I was pleasantly surprised to hear him talk about such goals, I wasn't convinced that he was ready. He didn't seem genuine, and it occurred to me that perhaps he was placating me with the college application talk so that I would agree to let him come home.

After the session, I asked Ben to show me the tunnels, which he was happy to do. We took the staircase to the bottom of the stairwell in Ben's dorm building, which dumped us in front of a well-built, slightly oversized door. On the other side, we stepped into the subterranean world of McLean Hospital, the bowels of the Asylum. Old fluorescent ceiling lights illuminated the chipped, yellowed paint inside the first tunnel. The plumbing pipes were exposed, and I was both fascinated and repulsed by these decrepit remains.

"Are you sure we can't get locked inside?" I asked before letting the door close.

"It's fine," he answered, showing me the full bars for reception on his cell phone.

Deeper into the tunnels I noticed several rooms with modern placards, which read ANIMAL FEED and ANIMAL TESTING. These doors had small windows, the kind with mesh wire in a diamond pattern you might see in old, thick, textured glass. Muted light shined from inside the rooms, and Ben explained that they were currently being used for research. We walked past several more locked rooms with DO NOT ENTER or RESTRICTED AREA signs posted on the doors. Ben veered towards the right, and I followed him down a tunnel that forked to the left.

"You know where we're going, right?" I asked.

"Yes," Ben replied with too much familiarity. "Just follow the arrows. This leads to the medical clinic and more labs and offices."

"Why do you like it here?" I wondered, feeling entombed by decay and past sorrows.

"I do the same therapy every day. I'm around the same people all day and night. Down here, I can be by myself. Once in a while I'll see someone go into one of the offices. I put on my headphones, listen to music, and pretend I'm somewhere else."

I didn't understand how the tunnels could be a pleasant experience, especially considering the spectacular foliage above ground, a beautiful, unexpected painting each day, rich with magentas, buttercups, bronzes, and corals. Why would Ben deprive himself of freedom or beauty? Why would anyone exile himself to meander through these nineteenth-century tunnels, which seemed to contain the memories of former patients, their horrifying secrets buried deep underground? I could almost hear their agonizing howls as they endured the painful jolts of seizures brought on by electroshock therapy. Ben's self-exile to roaming the tunnels provided a respite from a reality that he believed had forsaken him. The tunnels released him from the relentless disruption of punishing narratives that clawed at his being with deep, sharp talons like a bird of prey. Alone with his music, he found peace down there.

By the time I drove back to Southborough, I was listless. Each trip to McLean chipped away at the fiber of my being, like a mallet beating wood into pulp. I wished I could have walked away and left Ben and his secrets behind at McLean. Many nights in bed before falling asleep, I thought about leaving Massachusetts and returning to LA, but I could never leave him. He'd have no one to advocate for him, no one to care about him as much as I did.

After nineteen days at McLean, Ben was back on Wellbutrin. I was grateful for anything that reduced his cockamamie belligerence. Someone on his team must have realized this, too, and worked through this issue with him. Dr. Jenike was right; his team knew what they were doing, and Ben's success was contingent on his willingness to participate.

Family therapy on Thursday the 31st turned out to be our last session at McLean. Nate, Ben's behavior therapist, participated this time. Nate was a smart, no-nonsense kind of guy, young and impressive. He told me that he had offered Ben a mini-internship at the OCD Foundation offices in Boston, but Ben passed because it seemed "too boring." Nate listed a number of other scenarios he believed might move Ben to a more social and stimulating environment, only none of them piqued his interest. Nate's bottom line was that Ben was unwilling to continue therapy, and he couldn't help a patient who refused treatment. My heart sank that yet another opportunity was stolen by depression, anxiety, and OCD, as well as the reality that Ben would now be coming home.

"I'm terrified," I told Nate. "He's not ready to come home. I don't want him in my house like this. It's too painful." I was shocked at how easily these words came out of my mouth.

I will always remember Nate's response: "You have choices. You deserve to feel good in your home. If he's unwilling to contribute to that environment, he shouldn't be allowed to live there. If you tell him to leave and he won't, call the police. It's Ben's responsibility, not yours, if he chooses to live on the streets. He hasn't hit rock bottom yet, and maybe that's what needs to happen."

Suddenly, Ben's churlish, condescending demeanor disappeared like vapor. His face softened with genuine concern about the potential consequences in his future. He seemed vulnerable, but not defeated. Nate had gotten through to him.

"I won't let that happen," Ben said with a somber certainty. "I'll keep doing my exercises at home," he promised, but Nate didn't seem convinced.

Though I didn't say it, I believed that Ben had already hit his rock bottom. After a two-week hold in a lockdown facility and a future where his only option was waiting to get into the OCDI at McLean, his prospects already seemed grim. He had abandoned his friends and would be coming home to a bleak outlook with no job, no scholarship, and no college.

Still, Nate's words were empowering, not only to Ben, but to me, as well. I, too, had choices, and now Ben understood that, if necessary, kicking him out was no longer a veiled threat. Ben was the only person responsible for his life, for his mental, emotional, and physical wellbeing.

After Nate left the room, Terry mentioned some release paperwork that Ben still needed to complete for her. "You know," she told me, "we're here for Ben if he needs us in the future."

"What do you mean?" I thought Ben had just been kicked out of there.

"Many people return to the OCDI. Some people have even stayed here three separate times. Residential therapy at the OCDI is very intense." I appreciated her sensitivity to what I then perceived as failure.

Ben had been at McLean for twenty-three days. I had hovered in Massachusetts the same amount of time, ensuring that this last, great effort to help him would be effective. It took twenty-three days before I understood that this experience wasn't about me at all. Ben had to live his life unencumbered by me, no matter what that life turned out to be, and this was an enormous realization.

On the flight back to Los Angeles, Ben reflected about his time at McLean and said he believed it had been of some value. "At least now I know that I can easily live with a roommate," he said with relief and a sense of accomplishment. Ben needed the McLean experience in order to rewire an OCD belief. The thought of his imperfect body being exposed while living in a dorm room with a stranger was apparently a much greater fear of his than any of us understood.

Unbeknownst to Steven and me at the time, Ben had been researching scholarships and even began working on several college applications while at McLean. True to his word, as soon as he returned home, he met with his high school counselor about uploading his transcript and the essays he had previously written to complete his college applications. This time around, he only applied to schools in Massachusetts.

After a breakdown, a brief imprisonment, and six weeks spent in two psychiatric facilities on two different coasts, Ben emerged and reclaimed his purpose. He was accepted into all three schools he applied to and enrolled in the one that provided the most prestigious science scholarship for molecular biology majors. Dr. Jenike, Nate, and the team at McLean provided Ben with the tools to develop insight. Ben had to choose how to live his life. I could do no more.

CHAPTER 12

LUNATIC FRINGE...
DR. LLOYD SEDERER

Life can only be understood backwards,
but it must be lived forwards.
—IMMANUEL KANT

I thought I'd be happy when we returned to Los Angeles. Our family would be united after a month apart, and Ben's life would no longer be unraveling before my eyes or snatched away by something wicked and more powerful than me. I had become asphyxiated by agonizing sadness for him, and I didn't recognize that, while I was watching and waiting for his life to change, mine had fallen apart.

I had forgotten how much I missed Steven's hugs and how good it felt just holding each other. He was waiting for us at the front door and ran out to greet us. As soon as I saw him, I buried my neck into his, clutching onto him like a monkey until I heard him laugh.

"It's okay, Pokey," he said. "You did a great job in Massachusetts, and now you're home." He kissed me and gently removed my clenched hands from his T-shirt. Massachusetts had been rough, an experience Steven couldn't possibly understand without having been there, even though we had spoken to each other several times a day.

We debriefed about the pleasant flight back to Los Angeles, and then he went to work in his studio so that I could indulge in my post-travel ritual. As soon as I returned home from any trip, I'd immediately begin washing my clothes, separating a pile for items that had to be brought to the dry cleaner. My suitcase would return to its place in the closet, and all the remnants of the trip would disappear within sixty minutes.

Ben went into his room, and Cooper wouldn't be home from school for several more hours. The house seemed unfamiliar and I felt awkward as I dragged myself upstairs to my bedroom. A pile of junk mail waited for me on the bureau, unopened. The answer machine wasn't blinking with any messages. Nothing of consequence required my attention.

Now what, I wondered, sitting on my bed and glancing around my bedroom. I looked outside the window at the mid-sized skyscrapers in Century City, thinking how quickly we can slide into feeling irrelevant, forgotten. I felt crappy and overall, unhealthy. I'd gained eleven pounds since Ben pulled out of going to college back in August, just three months ago. My thoughts were tangled, as if the neurons in my brain were stuck in webs of gossamer. I wanted my life to make sense, to flow again. Hoping a little music might help, I turned on my iPod, which had been programmed to shuffle.

What came up first was Leonard Bernstein conducting the New York Philharmonic's performance of "Somewhere" from his musical *West Side Story*. It's an intoxicating piece of music. There is an elegance of order, a delicate purposefulness to the composition and orchestration as if each note admires the one before and enthusiastically engages and waits for its time to contribute. I felt lost amidst the complexity of the many notes that had a vibrant purpose. There was no place for me in this song, and it therefore reinforced my sense of purposelessness.

No matter how many doctors admired my strength and intelligence, or expressed regard for my capabilities, their compliments about my forbearance were meaningless. Our family doctor once said to me, "You're only as happy as your least happy child." How true.

On this first day home, I was too despondent to check e-mail or even look at my computer. However, I received a text from our therapist, Chris. He had spoken to Nate from McLean and heard that Ben and I were due back home. He wanted to set up a meeting with me before he saw Ben. It was a powerful moment of synchronicity, because I was the one who needed help. I needed to untangle the past. I needed to heal, and here was someone who could help me. I arranged to see him the next day.

Chris was close to my age, fifty-six, and tall, with rimmed glasses, which made him appear slightly bookish. He usually wore jeans with a nice sweatshirt. Once, I noticed a tattoo on his arm, barely hidden by the sleeve of his T-shirt, something I didn't expect from a Swarthmore graduate and a University of Southern California graduate school professor. Chris was thoughtful, intelligent, and, similar to Dr. Jenike, therapy wasn't confined to the four walls in his office. He, too, made house calls for patients in crisis.

I never needed a preface when I began a session with Chris, and the day I met with him after coming home was no different. Always attentive, he calmly waited for me to talk as I sat down on a chair across from him. I tried to speak, but I felt my tears choking my throat.

"My relationship with Ben and the distance between us hurts so much," I began. "I don't understand his secrets, his stories, and I don't know how to move past this." Yes, we were home, and yes, Ben had been helped at McLean, but I didn't know what to believe anymore. The pattern of secrets and lying had become too entrenched.

"The way I see it is that Ben's intent wasn't to lie to you," Chris began. "He was trying to protect himself, and the lies became second nature to him." According to Chris, Ben shared these narratives with his friends and his family because it was easier for him to make up a story about his health, rather than confront something he didn't understand about his mind. Ruminating alone in his room day and night further reinforced his self-defeating thoughts.

As Chris explained, "Rumination is when someone thinks about a certain topic, such as a past regret or future worry, over and over again, until it becomes time-consuming, futile, and depressogenic itself."

The root of Ben's illness was in his head; maybe he didn't understand how the suffering imposed by mental illness was as real as suffering inflicted by physical illness. His anxiety would often manifest in physical symptoms, like pronounced skin rashes that even a dermatologist wasn't able to diagnose. I told Chris how exhausted I was from the turmoil, the detailed narratives Ben had concocted and his constant demands to see specialists to confirm or allay his fears about medical problems, physical problems. I had become Ben's accuser, telling him he needed help for his OCD, treating him like a petulant child for behavior that neither he nor I, at that time, could comprehend.

"I want him back," I sobbed.

"Look, I disagree with Nate," Chris said, much to my surprise. "I think Ben has hit rock bottom, but he has to want to gain insight. He has to want to work on his coping skills."

"Do you think he'll be okay?" I asked, my voice quivering.

Chris nodded. "I do, but it's up to him."

I felt sad after I left the session with Chris, but believed that he had helped me see things differently. I suddenly understood that Ben had no agenda to deceive me; instead, he had been placing all his mental and physical energy into enduring day after day in unrelenting pain.

As I drove home, I was shocked by a jolt of clarity, as if a lightning bolt had struck me. My family wasn't in despair; in fact, we were altogether better than we had been in many years. I couldn't do anything more for Cooper or Ben. They both had a full toolkit of support, and it would be their choice whether or not to use those tools. The time had come for me to get on with the business of living my life. Yet so much time had passed, I wasn't sure where or how to begin.

It wasn't long before my private breakdown enveloped me. I was prescribed an SSRI that seemed to help my depression; three weeks later, it was determined that I had to immediately discontinue taking it. Grapefruit-sized black and blue circles that looked like huge bruises had suddenly appeared all over my body. My doctor ran a blood test, which indicated that my vitamin K level was too low, off the charts. Had I so much as slivered my finger on a slice of paper, I could have bled to death, because Celexa—and apparently all SSRIs—interfered with my blood clotting. This was an unknown, or underreported side effect, so my physician had to send a letter to report my reaction to the drug to the pharmaceutical company and the American Psychiatric Association.

Not long after I stopped taking the pills, I began to wonder if bleeding to death from an SSRI would not have been such a bad end result. After all, one day I would die, and if I had my druthers, I didn't want my death to be painful. I had once felt so fortunate for all the resources available to us, until they were all depleted—until I was depleted. My grief was excruciating. I wore it on my sleeve like Hester Prynne's scarlet letter, and I never spoke of this punishment to anyone. I began to believe that I didn't want to endure any more, not like this. I tried to imagine whether or not I had it in me to drive my car off Mulholland Drive, but then realized that I could end up living in a near vegetative state instead, which would be so much worse than my present life.

When will this misery become my past? I'd wonder to myself as tears dripped down my cheek, and I'd silently cry myself to sleep. *Will I ever breathe with joy and feel my body again, or will I remain numb forever?* An enormous black cloud hung over my head and followed me everywhere like a shadow. I felt wilted, like I was fading, disintegrating. I needed this cloud behind me. My life force had spun so out of control that I no longer knew how to rein it in. The decade of darkness had taken more courage, strength, and love than I could have imagined I possessed. The mad race turned into a marathon, and the finish line seemed nowhere in sight.

Hospital bills continued to arrive from UCLA long after we returned home from McLean: and the McLean bills wouldn't be too far behind. The bills from UCLA NPI reminded me of that horrible experience; even worse, those painful memories were defined by a dollar cost per day. I wasn't overwhelmed by Blue Cross's initial rejection for his two-week hospital hold, mandated by the State of California and Resnick NPI. Instead, I was still reeling from the result of a hearing about which I hadn't been advised, consulted, or informed. Eventually, Blue Cross reversed the five-figure denial, but the onus was on me to make more calls and resubmit faxes of paperwork to various divisions at Blue Cross. The protracted process diminished the victories, and I envisioned myself in a casket, jammed with EOBs that were partially visible after the lid was sealed closed.

In my ongoing attempt to understand this lunacy, I discovered an article written by Dr. Lloyd Sederer, medical editor for the *Huffington Post*. Sederer is also medical director of the New York State Office of Mental Health, the country's largest state mental health system, and is considered the "chief psychiatrist" of New York State. Highly credentialed, Dr. Sederer also happens to be the former medical director and executive vice president of McLean Hospital. It really made me wonder:

Do all the rock stars of neuroscience make a cameo appearance at McLean at some point?

Dr. Lloyd Sederer is someone you want to know before you or a loved one is in crisis. His book *A Family Guide to Mental Health Care* is an essential primer in understanding mental illness, as well as navigating the mental health care system. Sederer not only shares his concern about the shameful inadequacies that plague this community, but he's also deep in the trenches, fighting for reform. I found Dr. Sederer's website, then sent an e-mail to the "Ask Dr. Lloyd" address. I continued grappling with how HIPAA privacy laws could benefit a patient in a psychiatric lockdown facility. Was it so crazy for a mother to want to be advised of a hearing that would sequester her from her son? Dr. Sederer responded to my e-mail almost immediately. He explained to me something obvious, but almost impossible to consider when your son is in lockdown and your family is in crisis.

Although HIPAA law prevented Dr. Geary from divulging case information about our son, the law didn't prevent him from listening to loving parents, who had information that could shed light on Ben's condition. Sederer believed that a professional clinician ought to be open to information that might provide insight and contribute to more appropriate treatment for his patient.

As someone who regularly speaks with mental health policy makers and government officials around the country, Dr. Sederer suggested I contact the Treatment Advocacy Center, TAC, a non-profit mental health alliance located in Virginia. The Center was founded in 1998 as an independent voice for reforming treatment laws nationwide and working towards bettering treatment options for people with severe mental illness. The Center provides both the public and policy makers with a reliable source of information about State treatment laws and supplies family members with information and resources for helping mentally ill loved ones.

Dr. Sederer believes wholeheartedly that recovery from mental illness is possible, and that hope is the driver from crisis into recovery. One of my favorite quotes from Sederer's book *A Guide to Mental Health Care* bolstered my hope, my belief in myself, and in my sons' ability to get well:

> "Trust your instincts," he urges. "To do the right thing, you must face the unwanted visitor of mental illness and act before it defeats the person you love—and you as well."

For me, hope had been drifting in and out of my days, almost taunting me, unable to find a fixed place in my mind. Weeks became months, then years, and then a decade. Through this time, it was impossible for me to imagine that this unyielding eclipse would dissipate and fade into my past. I was so intent on wishing my life away that I almost missed noticing when the sun finally appeared.

Suddenly, our lives began to glisten. I vividly remember a particularly special day when Cooper and I were in the car together, driving back from the Disney lot. Cooper had entered and won a contest to attend a VIP event for the upcoming release of the next *Kingdom Hearts* video game.

"I've been noticing something different about myself," he began. "I smile all the time. I wonder why?" This random observation wasn't typical of Cooper, but I was thrilled he said it out loud to me.

Of course, I had noticed how much he had changed, how much more at ease he was with himself, how much more we laughed together. At 17, Cooper had matured, and his tics no longer interfered with his life. He felt happiness again, a feeling he hadn't experienced since he'd turned seven years old—the year that marked his life AT, *After Tourette's*. As I continued driving, he actually thanked me for taking him to UCLA every week so that he could learn CBIT; for helping him practice his breathing exercises at night.

Then, one of my dreams came true: Cooper made it through high school. We were all so proud of him at his graduation; he had a mini fan club, wildly applauding when he took to the stage to receive his diploma and the dean announced he had graduated with honors.

After being home from McLean for five months, Ben surprised us with a part-time job he secured, working in a frame store. He enrolled in a Photoshop class at UCLA Extension. Although his plan was to go to college in August, I wasn't yet convinced. After all, we had tried this once before.

CHAPTER 13

KISS PAST GOOD-BYE...
DR. JON KABAT-ZINN

Nothing is worth more than this day.
—JOHAN WOLFGANG VON GOETHE

I had become disconnected from feelings of jubilation, so I was uncharacteristically slow to react when, in January, we received the incredible news: both Ben and Cooper were accepted into the university of their choice. This news became the catalyst for my transformation. For the first time in more than a decade, my family wasn't in crisis. I was so overjoyed for us all, and I was ready to make my commitment to wellness.

I had lost so much of my life by not being present, by not knowing what was going on in so many past moments. Determined not to waste so many future moments, I enrolled in a 6-week online class with UCLA's Mindfulness Awareness Research Center, MARC. I knew that I wouldn't be comfortable just sitting on my floor meditating, so I shopped online for a Zafu meditation cushion stuffed with buckwheat, which conforms to your posture like sand on a beach. The beige, crescent moon-shaped pillow arrived, and fit nicely in my office.

The class had a syllabus and guided meditations each week from Diana Winston, based on the inspiring book she co-wrote with Dr. Susan Smalley, *Fully Present: The Science, Art, and Practice of Mindfulness*. The fourteen members in the class from all across the country participated in weekly online chats, moderated by our instructor, so that we could share our experiences. It was incredible how quickly our group of strangers bonded, how openly we expressed deeply personal reactions to various meditations. We learned as a class that when we practice mindfulness, our thoughts become dim, our narratives tune out; instead, we are simply in the present moment. No *"What If"* thoughts or worries about the future or the past.

Mindfulness means maintaining a moment-by-moment awareness of our thoughts, feelings, bodily sensations, and surrounding environment. By focusing on our breathing, this natural rhythm moves our lives forward, moment by moment. We become aware of our thoughts and feelings without judging them—without believing, for instance, that there's a "right" or "wrong" way to think or feel in a given moment. Our thoughts and emotions are fleeting and do not define us, an insight that can break negative thought patterns. Although we did the daily meditation practice at home, the online chats and reminder texts we would send each other made us feel so connected, as a group.

Dr. Jon Kabat-Zinn is Professor of Medicine Emeritus and creator of the Stress Reduction Clinic and the Center for Mindfulness in Medicine, Health Care, and Society at the University of Massachusetts Medical School. In 1980, he pioneered the Mindfulness Based Stress Reduction program (MBSR), which is today offered by medical centers, hospitals, and health maintenance organizations across the country. The decades-long empirical research of Kabat-Zinn and many others have proven

MBSR benefits for psoriasis, pain, anxiety, depression, brain function, and immune function. His first book, *Full Catastrophe Living: Using the Wisdom of Your Body and Mind to Face Stress, Pain, and Illness*, is a mindfulness primer, a step-by-step approach to MBSR.

According to Kabat-Zinn, "Mindfulness is awareness that arises through paying attention, on purpose, in the present moment, nonjudgmentally." In simpler terms, "It's about knowing what is going on your mind." He further explains, "The practice of mindfulness ...is not used in the common sense of 'rehearsal' for some future performance. The performance is always this moment unfolding." What is becomes what was, and this moment is fresh—it's new, it's my now, my present, and my life.

Mindfulness requires commitment, and, I think, the practice must be taught. I've discovered that meditation has helped balance my perspective about what's going on in my life at a given moment. Meditation has helped remove the past clutter of narratives or judgments that never served me. Feeling sad about the past certainly didn't make me more productive. Yet each new moment, each new breath became another opportunity for feeling whole and grateful. I knew that my mind and body needed mindfulness as my intervention for wellness; which is why, after the online class ended, I registered for Diana Winston's daylong retreat at UCLA called, "Mindfulness, Self-compassion, and our Shared Humanity."

Although my sister, Dani, wasn't really into meditation, I invited her to join me because who couldn't benefit from a day of self-compassion? I was thrilled when she agreed to be my guest for this seminar. Essentially, we spent the day in silence—after all, this was about meditation. However, during the walking meditation exercise, outside on the quad, it was impossible not to hear Dani laughing under her breath, observing 200 people walking like zombies, in slow motion, expressionless faces deep in concentration. I turned away to pass her, because I nearly broke the silence with my inimitable cackle. The day flew by, and we both had an awesome experience.

Mindfulness has helped me create distance between my thoughts and feelings. By being present, in the moment, without judgment, I can disassociate biased, learned beliefs and think beyond those limits. In James Joyce's collection of stories, *The Dubliners*, he describes Duffy, the main character in one story called "A Painful Case":

> "He lived a little distance from his body, regarding his own acts with doubtful side glances."

The distance Joyce described was the same distance I have had to reflect on the past—acknowledging old thoughts, but not needing to hold onto them. Yes, much in my recent past was heinous; but here, in this present moment, I am grateful and motivated. I'm learning to be kind to myself, and to let go of past anger and sorrow. Practicing mindfulness, releasing old thoughts, has expanded my awareness; this shift in consciousness has helped me understand that this moment isn't just about me. The whole universe, and everything in it, conspires to make each moment happen—for every one of us.

Jon Kabat-Zinn is my present rock star. I'm healing, and I experience tremendous benefit from meditation, and just being. As long as I can breathe, I can live in each present moment; and breathing unconditional loving kindness and compassion is available to me anytime, anywhere. Love is the essence of what makes us human—it surrounds us and sustains us through crisis.

The synchronicities throughout my life, when they occurred, brought my attention to my then-present thoughts and feelings. This sense of synchronicity reflects a shift in consciousness and awareness, which reveals the power of our connection, our shared humanity. I'll be working on being mindful for the rest of my life, because being conscious matters to me. Loving and being loved matters to me, and connecting with a purpose greater than myself gives me a reason to wake up every morning.

I had spent too much time on a harrowing journey without a guide, without a roadmap and every sharp turn we took accentuated my weak navigation skills. I'd often become lost. I'd become overwhelmed with anguish, witnessing the tremendous agony and suffering of the people I loved so much.

I couldn't have imagined that one day I would be getting both kids ready to move onto college campuses, on opposite sides of the country; but that day arrived in August 2014. Ben had to be at freshman orientation on the East Coast two weeks before Cooper's orientation date in California. This was perfect because I could help both of them move into their respective dorms and be part of this humongous transition. Shopping for school and dorm supplies for Cooper was a piece of cake. He didn't even need to shop for new clothes. As he said, "Mum, I'll be an hour away. I'll come home if I need anything."

Ben, on the other hand, *the minimal man*, agreed to shop for essentials...bare-bones necessities. He already had his laptop and cell phone. He bought a package of pens, pencils, erasers, notebooks, bedding, towels, and a rain slicker.

"Don't you think it would be a good idea to have a pair of winter boots?" I asked, standing in the mall outside of Macy's waiting for his answer.

"No, I don't want any boots," he stated.

Good grief, I thought. *He's been in Boston during many cold, snowy winters. He always wore boots.* Not willing to argue about survival basics, I figured this was an item he could purchase after the first big storm.

"Well, you need long jeans, or khakis, or some kind of long pants, right?" I continued trying to engage Ben in the shopping for college process. He reluctantly agreed, and we returned home with what I called his "starter wardrobe."

Preparing Ben for his move was like pulling taffy; I held on to the hope that the sweet result would be worth the struggle. Shopping, and packing boxes to ship to his school in time for his arrival began to stress him out; and knowing that we'd be flying back to Boston, alone, together, I decided to acquiesce. He could easily buy whatever he needed online once he was at school. Unlike most parents, who become caught up in the frenzy of dorm décor, I had only one item on my to-do list: *just get Ben to school.*

In discussing travel arrangements, Ben preferred to take the red eye flight, arriving in Boston on Sunday morning, the day of freshman orientation. He'd have one day to prepare for his first semester, which commenced on Monday.

My initial reaction to his preference was not very mindful. "Are you crazy? You'll be too exhausted to dive right into unpacking and orientation, and then starting class on Monday!" I was still plagued by the shocking events of the previous year, and felt some uncertainty about Ben attending school.

My son asked me to calm down and hear him out, which I did. He explained that flying in on Saturday, with the dormant time spent in a hotel room overnight with me, would cause him more anxiety than flying in and going straight to his school. I reminded myself that this was his experience, so I followed his direction. He expressed what he needed to feel okay and demonstrated his engagement by planning the itinerary, booking our flights, and printing out our boarding passes.

After we arrived at his school, a team of students was available to help him move into his dorm. His roommate, Jason, and his parents, had already finished unpacking. Jason was from Ohio, a geology major whose father happened to be one of the country's leading researchers studying emerging adults with autism, and transitions and opportunities available to this population post high school. *I'm always on the lookout for rock stars of neuroscience, and this seemed like another coincidence to me. It made me feel as though there were people everywhere working to help us understand the brain.*

Their room was rather small and the hot, humid weather made the space feel even stuffier. It wasn't long before Ben was ready for me to leave—he hadn't even unpacked his things. I kissed him good-bye, and told him how proud I was of him. I would not look back with any thought other than he's where he chose to be. I was thrilled for him...for both of us.

By contrast, moving Cooper into his dorm was relatively easy—and much more comfortable. His large, 4-person suite included air conditioning. Cooper wanted us to stay just long enough for Steven to help him hook up his television, computer, and his PlayStation 3. He didn't want a kiss, but we managed a quick hug sandwich. Steven and I told him how incredibly proud we were of this accomplishment, and that the best was yet to come.

Two weeks into being empty nesters and I was LOVING IT! Steven, however, immediately felt lonely without the boys being around. He had quickly forgotten the morning ritual, being interrogated by Attila the Hun.

"Dad, please don't *schmatz* your banana!" Yes, Cooper was much better, but I wanted Steven to appreciate our new freedom from his imposing sensitivities.

The thing that disturbed Steven the most was that Ben hadn't called him from school, nor did he return his calls, and the one time they had spoken in these last two weeks, Ben had been abrupt. Steven wanted to hear his son's voice, hear how things were going with his roommate, his classes, and his thoughts about his professors. Instead, after a brief exchange, Ben interjected, "I have to get to my class, Dad. Love you. Bye." *Click.*

After three weeks, I discovered that when I'd text Ben, he'd respond. Poor Steven, unwilling to abandon his flip phone, he hadn't yet experienced this brave new world of smartphones and emojis. I had decided to cut Ben some slack after learning that he was taking five classes; plus, the 3-hour time difference was an additional inconvenience, in terms of phone calling. Unlike Steven, I felt as connected to Ben as I had expected to be. Although his texts were minimal, there were never any complaints. *It doesn't get better than this*, I thought.

By the two-month mark, however, Ben had shared so little about his life at school that I, too, fell prey to the more dominant feelings of concern about his future, and ill-fated memories from the previous year. *Anything could happen.*

At the end of October, Ben called one night to wish me a happy birthday.

"Mom, go open the front door," he instructed.

"Why, Ben? It's dark outside."

Of course I did as he instructed, turned on the lights, and saw a box under the doorbell. Ben had sent me flowers for my birthday, a dozen yellow roses, my favorite—the first real birthday gift I'd ever received just from him. Yet, the best part of my birthday gift was when he told me that he was happy at school, and wouldn't want to be at any other university—as an undergraduate. And that moment became our turning point; I knew then that Ben would be okay. I told Cooper about the flowers and he was really pleased for me that Ben "sucked it up and did the right thing."

Closer to winter break when Ben called (it was usually because he needed money) I heard that long-forgotten sound of the warmth in his voice. He began talking about medical school, and reclaiming a future life. Cooper had found his passion earlier in the year. As a freshman, he became secretary of the Anime Club. "I should be able to become president of the club by my junior year," he explained, navigating the college politics of becoming a club officer.

I could never have imagined last August that in May I'd be thinking, *I can't wait for them to come home*—but I'm excited beyond belief. I'd expect them both to be in therapy for a summer tune-up because I've learned that transitions, both good and bad, can be taxing for those with OCD. Besides, this was now about them being in recovery, not crisis.

I, too, reclaimed my life, which began with practicing mindfulness. I wanted meaningful work, I wanted to help others, and I wanted to be surrounded by close friends and family, the people with whom I shared great love.

Although I might not have been aware of it at the time, the deeper our crises became, the stronger my love sustained me for whoever needed it most. We are meant to love, and be loved; it's in our DNA. Imagine that we have two hearts: one is the muscle in our chest, the engine that supplies the physical means for our body to work efficiently. It makes sense that our heart is a muscle because it expands like a rubber balloon and has the capacity to contain an entire lifetime of experiences. The second is a shadow heart, which we cannot see because it lives deep within our brain; it's the soul of the heart, the essence of everything. Love is this essence, and common to every human being; it is enduring and powerful.

The many kindnesses of people throughout my life, some of whom I've never even met, have proven to me that love is abundant. It's strong, but if you don't use it, you can lose it: there is no place for love in a fearful heart. Anxiety creates the fear and uncertainty, which blocks empathy and closes the heart. Without empathy we are lost, alone, and unable to connect to each other.

Love is inside us all. It's what makes us human, and to quote Jon Kabat-Zinn, "It's available any time we call upon it." Each day I try to create some happy, meaningful moments. Often, I'll go out for a walk and bring my iPhone, headphones, and a piece of bubble gum. I enjoy listening to my music slightly louder than average, and I love it when the track shuffles to my favorite Van Halen song, "Right Now":

> *Right now, hey*
> *It's your tomorrow*
> *Right now,*
> *C'mon, it's everything*
> *Right now,*
> *Catch that magic moment, do it*
> *Right here and now*
> *It means everything*
> *It's enlightened me, right now*
> *What are you waiting for*

EPILOGUE, OR GRAVITY...
DR. ANTHONY ROTHSCHILD

I n its most simple sense, survival is recovery, and as such, recovery is an ongoing action, a conscious awareness that our moment-to-moment selves are present, and an assurance that our hearts and minds won't become lost or stolen from us ever again. Recovery requires vigilance because if we aren't aware of what's happening in our lives, or in our minds, relapse is ready to pounce. Like a pesky mosquito sucks your blood, relapse will suck out your soul.

In the fall of 2015 I saw the devastation of relapse, and understood that maintaining recovery is as challenging as overcoming crisis. Ben expected his return to university to be even more fulfilling than the previous year. After all, as a sophomore he knew what to anticipate academically, and this time, he even knew his roommates. Ben and I took a red eye to Boston, and I dropped him off at school at 7:00 a.m. on Saturday. He was looking forward to getting settled into his suite.

I had planned to visit my best friend, who lived in Manchester-by-the-Sea in Massachusetts, about ninety minutes away from Ben. I arrived at Cece's house, unpacked my things, and joined my dear friend outside on her deck. It was perfection, luxuriating in the tranquility of being in an old, New England home overlooking the Atlantic Ocean, surrounded by trees, with cardinals chirping in the quiet air.

The two-word phone text—*"I'm sad"*—began on Monday morning. Frenetic phone calls began to launch on Tuesday, bombarding my cell phone every four hours. Ben's voice escalated like a rocket. "I can't be here! I can't be in this building! I have to leave; I have to defer this semester. It's awful, and I can't do this!"

Good grief, I thought. *This can't be happening again.* What possibly could have transpired from Saturday morning to Tuesday to cause this unforeseen calamity?

"Mom, I can't be here. I've been adding and dropping classes, and now I can't get in to the classes I need."

"Okay, so go talk to your professors. They love you, they'll understand a class change, right?"

"You don't get it. I can't be in my room; I haven't slept since I got here. I feel sick."

"Ben, you just had a three-month break. You saw Chris all summer, and I don't get what's going on. It sounds like you're having a panic attack." Before I could ask if he had taken a pill for his anxiety, he refuted that allegation.

"No, it's not a panic attack! I can't be here now, I can't think, I can't concentrate. I waited too long, and for one class that I need for core, the professor couldn't let me in."

"Okay, let's be calm for a moment. It's only the third day of classes, right?"

"Four as of tomorrow," he interjected.

"There must be other core options. Go through the list of classes that are still open, and find one, just to have a complete schedule. Doesn't that make sense?" I suggested calmly.

"I guess so," he agreed, but sounded as though he still needed convincing.

"Ben, just talk to your advisor, finalize an approved schedule, so you'll have a roadmap, and know your academic plan. Okay?" I tried to sound upbeat, but didn't want Ben to think that I was minimizing his struggle.

Over the next several days, the momentum of his irrational calls increased to every several hours—alternating between calling me in Massachusetts and calling Steven, who had just taken Cooper back to school in Los Angeles. The strangest thing about Ben's plan was that he wanted to defer just a semester, not the whole year. He didn't want to transfer, because he liked the school.

By Friday night, the all-too-familiar fractured narratives returned, with omissions that were customized for his calls with Steven and with me. I got stories that he could never catch up from his missed classes and tests, he was only registered for three classes, a calculus class he didn't need, a psychology class, and an art class. He missed two psych lectures, slept through his math class, and now his GPA was destroyed; he'd never get into med school. Steven got that someone posted on an internal website something private and embarrassing about him, though it had since been taken down. "But people remember those posts," Ben was quick to emphasize. He further added that he was being teased and harassed. Ben would never tell me a story like that because he knows I have no tolerance for bullies. I suspected, though I didn't know for certain, that Ben knew I would leave no stone unturned if a son of mine was harassed in school. No, this was far-fetched in my mind.

Unlike Steven, I had moved beyond Ben's detailed narratives. They were, to me, "*tales told by an idiot, full of sound and fury, and signifying nothing...*" in a Shakespearean sense. My more mindful self was focused only on the fact that Ben needed mental health care; that's what mattered. My goal was to get him in to a shrink, someone who could assess him and help us decide what to do.

I spent the next several days making calls. First, I spoke to Chris in Los Angeles. I needed his guidance, because I had no idea what kind of help Ben needed. Was this OCD, a panic attack, depression?

"He didn't open up all summer," Chris began. "I agree with you," he said without hesitation. "There's no value to him returning to LA. He'll continue to isolate. By staying there, being around other kids, this could be a golden opportunity for Ben to confront whatever's been simmering these last few years."

I was relieved to hear Chris say this, because I knew that Ben coming home was not the answer. He'd just stay in his room, isolate, and have nothing to do for four months. Next, I spoke to Nate, his therapist from the McLean OCDI, and that was the moment when I knew that Nate had been right after all: *Ben hadn't hit rock bottom—until now.* Considering I thought that Ben had been kicked out of McLean, Nate was awesome, and both he and Diane Davey were so generous in making recommendations and spending time trying to find help for Ben. I called anyone I could think of who might know of a therapist in western Massachusetts. I contacted people I didn't know, like Jeff Bell, the head of the OCD Foundation, as part of my S.O.S.

Over the weekend, I made it clear to Ben that after speaking with both Chris and Nate, coming home for several months was not an option—which sent him reeling.

"You saw Chris all summer, avoided taking meds, and I don't want to spend time arguing. I'm here to help you, Ben," I reminded him. "But there's not much I can do unless you want to live, unless you want to fight and help yourself."

"What should I do?" he asked with complete authenticity. He had no idea what he should try next.

"You need to make an emergency appointment with a mental health counselor there, on campus," I said. "I think there's a special number for her extension."

"Okay, I'll call," he agreed.

But I also promised that I wouldn't leave Massachusetts until we found someone who could help him, which was no easy task. There simply are too few psychiatrists—especially for kids on college campuses. Besides, I knew that Ben required more than a bi-weekly chat with an on-campus therapist. I contacted two shrinks and one therapist in the area; none of them were taking on new patients. Undeterred, I remembered that I'd found another rock star at University of Massachusetts Medical School, a name I saved just in case Ben needed to see someone when he was a freshman.

Dr. Anthony Rothschild has spent more than 25 years in clinical psychopharmacology and psychoneuroendocrinology treating patients with depression. His specialty was studying the diagnostic challenges, biology, course, and treatment of this disorder. He is on the Editorial Board of the *Journal of Clinical Psychiatry, Depression, and Anxiety*, and was honored with the Massachusetts Psychiatric Society Outstanding Psychiatrist Award for Research. Rothschild is the editor of the *Evidenced-Based Guide to Antidepressant Medication*. Of course, he did his psychiatry residency at McLean Hospital/Harvard Medical School.

His assistant returned my call on Tuesday, and explained that Dr. Rothschild only sees patients who are part of his clinical trials. I don't know why, but for some reason I figured that making an appointment with Dr. Rothschild would be a slam-dunk; unfortunately, unlike the other specialists I had called, who had private practices, Rothschild was part of a research and teaching university medical school associated with a hospital. He didn't have a private practice. My heart sank. I explained to her that my son attended a nearby school and that he was from Los

Angeles. He desperately needed help. I asked if she could recommend someone, anyone, for Ben to see, and explained that he couldn't even see a therapist at his school until Friday. She offered to speak with Dr. Rothschild, and asked me to call her back late Friday morning.

Poor Ben had suffered a week, tormented by a brain that continued to undermine him. I couldn't imagine what it must have been like for him, waiting another two days to see a campus therapist on Friday. Ben called me after his session.

"Mom, I need someone to talk to, not just a counselor," he whimpered on the phone.

I ached for Ben, because after these many years, he seemed to finally want help, only now, help was so elusive.

"Ben, Dad and I love you so much. I promise I will not leave Massachusetts until we find you good care.

He didn't say anything for a few seconds. "I love you," he said, a phrase he hadn't expressed all summer.

"You deserve to be happy, Ben," I continued. "This must be so hard for you. Promise to hang in there. You will get better." I believed these words I said to Ben, because I felt his anguish, and knew that this time, he wanted to be well.

I thought about Ben's behavior over the summer, and how I kept asking him if he wanted to get away, perhaps do something fun before he had to go back to school. Cooper invited him to go to a taping of one of his favorite television shows, *The Voice*, but he opted out. Ben didn't seem particularly sad or mad over the summer; it was more like he turned off his happiness switch. We came to accept this as Ben's adolescent personality; he had been like this since senior year in high school.

On Friday morning I called Dr. Rothschild's office and his assistant, Nancy, told me that the doctor was currently recruiting for a clinical trial for depression. Ben might be a good candidate, and if he were accepted into the trial, he would become Dr. Rothschild's patient. The next step was for Ben himself to call one of trial clinicians to be pre-screened. Nancy explained that too often parents try to get their kid into a trial, and then the son or daughter doesn't want to participate. I assured her that she would be hearing from Ben.

I texted Ben with the news, and told him he had to call the doctor's office immediately if he wanted to be considered for this trial. A leading anxiety and depression specialist would assess him. Ben phoned me after he spoke with the clinician and said he really liked her, and the call went well. It was a starting point, a glimmer of hope. He had an appointment to be interviewed for the trial. I felt so proud of him for making the call, and wanted to believe that this time, he was ready to take responsibility for his choices, and his life. But the memories from the past were still too recent.

The following Wednesday, I rented a car to drive from Cece's house to take Ben to his intake appointment at U Mass. Medical School in Worcester. Ben told me that the intake investigator explained that he might be there for three to four hours. His assessment would include a complete medical history, blood work, and an EKG. After two hours of answering questions and having every detail of the trial clearly explained to him, Ben agreed to participate. I was then asked to wait in the hallway while they conducted his physical.

Suddenly, the large hallway door opened and Dr. Rothschild came out to talk to me. "You know," he began, "your son is very depressed. He has major depressive disorder (MDD). But I want you to know, as I told him, depression is very common. Doctors, lawyers, artists, bankers—many people learn that they can manage their depression and lead full lives."

I looked at him and suddenly realized that Ben had a doctor, a rock star, to help him through this nightmare. Before I could say anything, Dr.

Rothschild continued, "I think he'll do well on this medication. And if not, we'll find something that will help him. We'll be here for Ben."

I stood up and thought about doing pirouettes down the hall to hug this sweet, kind man, but I restrained myself. I kept smiling at him as his words resonated in my head. *"We'll be here for Ben."* Everyone who suffers from depression needs to hear those words; they need to know that people care, and will try to help them. They need to know that they are not alone.

References

Chapter 1

International Headache Society in Cephalalgia (2004): *The International Classification of HeadacheDisorders*: (2nd ed.). Cluster Headache and other Trigeminal Autonomic Cephalalgias.Vol. 24 Suppl 1:9-160.

Láinez M. (2015). American Academy of Neurology (AAN) 67th Annual Meeting. *Hope for Suicide Headache.* Medscape. May 05, 2015.

Transcendental meditation. (n.d.) *Mosby's Medical Dictionary*, (8th ed.). (2009).

Yogi, M.M. (1976). *Science of Being and Art of Living: Transcendental Meditation.* (8th edition). London: MIU Press.

Chapter 2

American Psychiatric Association. (May 1994). *Diagnostic and Statistical Manual of MentalDisorders (DSM).* (4th ed.). Arlington, VA: American Psychiatric Publishing. Diagnostic criteria Asperger's.

American Psychiatric Association. (May 2013). *Diagnostic and Statistical Manual of MentalDisorders (DSM)*. (5th ed.). Arlington, VA: American Psychiatric Publishing. Diagnostic criteria Asperger's/ASD.

Baron-Cohen, MD, S. (9 November 2009). The Short Life of a Diagnosis. *New York Times*.

Baron-Cohen, MD, S. (2008). *Autism and Asperger Syndrome (The Facts Series)*. Oxford: Oxford University Press.

Cassidy, S., Bradley, P., Robinson, J., Allison, C., McHugh, M., & Baron-Cohen, S. (June 2014). Suicidal ideation and suicide plans or attempts in adults with Asperger's syndrome attending a specialist diagnostic clinic: a clinical cohort study. *Lancet Psychiatry*.
Retrieved http://dx.doi.org/10.1016/S2215-0366(14)70248-2.

University of California-Irvine. (March 2006). Researchers Identify New Form of Superior Memory Syndrome. *Science Daily*. Retrieved www.sciencedaily.com/releases/2006/03/060314085102.

Peek, F., & Hanson, L. (2007). *The Life and Message of The Real Rain Man: The Journey of a Mega-Savant*. Dude Publishing/National Professional Resources, Inc.

MENSA. www.mensa.org.

Chapter 3

Hoffman, A. (April 1, 1983). *LSD My Problem Child: Reflections on Sacred Drugs, Mysticism, and Science*. Los Angeles, CA: J. P. Tarcher.

Lilly, J. C., Austin, G. M., & Chambers, W. W. (July 1952). Threshold movements produced by excitation of cerebral cortex and efferent fibers with some parametric regions of rectangular current pulses (cats and monkeys). *Journal of Neurophysiology.* 15(4), 319-41. PMID 14955703.

Lilly, J. C., Hughes J.R., Alvord, E.C. Jr, Galkin, T.W. (April 1955). Brief, Noninjurious Electric Waveform for Stimulation of the Brain. *Science.* 121(3144), 468-469. Retrieved doi:10.1126/science.121.3144.468.

Lilly, J.C. (1956). Mental Effects of Reduction of Ordinary Levels of Physical Stimuli on Intact, Healthy Persons. *Psychiatric Research Reports.* 5, pp. 1-9.

Lilly, John C. 1958. "Rewarding and Punishing Systems in the Brain" in The Central Nervous System and Behavior. Transactions of the First Conference, Josiah Macy, Jr., Foundation, Princeton, N.J. (L.C. 59-5052.) P. 247-303.

Lilly, John C. 1959. " 'Stop' and 'Start' Effects in The Central Nervous System and Behavior." Transactions of the Second Conference, Josiah Macy, Jr., Foundation and National Science Foundation, Princeton, N.J. (L.C. 59-5052.) P. 56-112

Lilly MD, J. C., Montagu, A. (13 October 1963). Modern Whales, Dolphins and Porpoises, as Challenges to Our Intelligence. *The Dolphin in History.* A Symposium given at the William Andrews Clark Memorial Library, Univ. of California. Los Angeles, CA: University of California Press. P. 31-54. http://dx.doi.org/10.5962/bhl.title.7289.

Lilly MD, John C. (1965). "Dolphin-Human Relationship and LSD-25." Abramson, H. Ed; Fremont-Smith, F. Intro. *Second International Conference* on the Use of LSD in Psychotherapy and Alcoholism. Indianapolis, IN: The Bobbs-Merrill Co., Inc. P. 47-52

Lilly MD, J. C. (1967). The Mind of the Dolphin: A Non-Human Intelligence. New York, NY: Doubleday & Co.

Lilly MD, J.C. (1985). The Center of the Cyclone: An Autobiography of Inner Space. (3rd ed.). New York, NY: Julian Press.

Barrus, I., Vletas, S. (January 2003). Restricted Environmental Stimulation Technique (R.E.S.T.). Alterations of Consciousness: An Empirical Analysis for Social Scientists. Washington, DC: American Psychological Association (APA); p.45.

Chapter 4

Tyler, S. (1973). Dream On. [Recorded by Aerosmith] Aerosmith. [CD]. New York, NY: Columbia Records. BMG Rights Management, US.

Hagler, M. (13 March 2013). "Division-By-Division"—The Greatest Fighters of All-Time. Boxrec.com.

[Tyler, S., Perry, J.] (1985). My Fist Your Face. [Recorded by Aerosmith] Done With Mirrors. Los Angeles, CA: Geffen Records. Sony/ATV Music Publishing LLC, Warner/Chappell Music, Inc.

Ogunnaike, L. (11 July 2004). The Shrinking of the American Band. New York Times. Music.

Friedman, A.K., Walsh, J.J. Juarez, B., Ku S.M., Chaudhury, D., Wang, J.... Han, M.H. (18 April 2104). Enhancing depression mechanisms in midbrain dopamine neurons achieves homeostatic resilience. *Science,* 344, 313-9. 344(6181):313-9. doi:10.1126/science.1249240.

Chaudhury, D., Walsh, J. J., Friedman, A. K., Juarez, B., Ku, S. M., Koo, J. W., … Han M.H.(12 December 2012). Rapid regulation of depression-related behaviors by control of midbrain dopamine neurons. *Nature.*

Keltner, D. (8 January 2009). *Born to Be Good: The Science of A Meaningful Life.* New York, NY: W. W. Norton & Company.

Piff, P., & Keltner, D. (May 24, 2015). Why Do We Experience Awe? *New York Times,* Sunday Review, p. SR10.

American Psychiatric Association. (27 May 2013). *Diagnostic and Statistical Manual of Mental Disorders (DSM).* (5th ed.). Arlington, VA: Substance Addiction.

Chapter 5

Leary, T. (1957). *Interpersonal Diagnosis of Personality.* New York, NY: The Ronald Press Company.

Leary, T. (December 1958). Interpersonal Diagnosis of Personality. *American Journal of Physical Medicine and Rehabilitation.* 37(6), 331.

Leary, T., Metzner, A, & Alpert, R. (1964). *The Psychedelic Experience: A Manual Based on the Tibetan Book of the Dead.* New Hyde Park, NY: University Books.

Kansra, N., & Shih, C. W. (21 May 2012). Harvard LSD Research Draws National Attention. *The Harvard Crimson.*

American Psychiatric Association. (May 1994). *Diagnostic and Statistical Manual of Mental Disorders (DSM).* (4th ed.). Arlington, VA: Tourette Syndrome.

American Psychiatric Association. (27 May 2013). *Diagnostic and Statistical Manual of Mental Disorders (DSM).* (5th ed.). Arlington, VA: Tourette Syndrome.

Chapter 6

Piacentini, PhD, J., Woods, PhD, D. W., Scahill, PhD, MSN, L., Wilhelm, PhD, S., Peterson, PhD, A. L., Chang, PhD, S., . . . Walkup, MD, J. T. (2010). Behavior Therapy for Children With Tourette Disorder, A Randomized Controlled Trial. *JAMA.* 303(19), 1929-1937. doi:10.1001/jama.2010.607.

Leckman, J. F., Walker, D. E., & Cohen, D. J. (1993). Premonitory urges in Tourette's syndrome. *Am. J. Psychiatry.* 150(1), 98-102.

Himle, M. B., Woods, D. W., Piacentini, J. C., & Walkup, J. (2006). Brief review of habit reversal training for Tourette's syndrome. *J Child Neurol.* 21(8), 719-725.

The Tourette Association of America (TAA). www.tourette.org.
The TAA is the driving force in scientific and clinical progress relevant to TS.

Chapter 7

Mansueto, PhD, C. S. (2014). Behavior Therapy Center of Greater Washington. Retrieved https://iocdf.org/wp-content/uploads/2014/09/Tourette.

Section 504 is a federal law.

The Section 504 regulations require a school district to provide a "free appropriate public education" (FAPE) to each qualified student with a disability who is in the school district's jurisdiction, regardless of the nature or severity of the disability. Under Section 504, FAPE consists of the provision of regular or special education and related aids and services designed to meet the student's individual educational needs as adequately as the needs of nondisabled students are met.

Retrieved http://www2.ed.gov/about/offices/list/

The Individuals with Disabilities Education Act (IDEA) requires education institutions, in collaboration with parents (and older students), to tailor an individualized education program (IEP) for each student with a disability that meets the unique needs of that student.

Retrieved http://www2.ed.gov/programs/specediep/in

Eddy, C. M., & Cavanna, A. E. (November 2013). It's a curse!: coprolalia in Tourette syndrome. *Eur J Neurol*. 20(11), 1467-70. Epub 7 June 2013. doi:10.1111/ene.12207.

Dion, LSWA, P. N. (16 May 2007). Retrieved www.misophonia.com.

Greene, R. (20 May 2014). *The Explosive Child: A New Approach for Understanding and Parenting Easily Frustrated, Chronically Inflexible Children.* (5 Rev Upd ed.). New York, NY: Harper Paperbacks.

Greene, PhD., R.
Retrieved www.cpsconnection.com; www.LivesintheBalance.com.

Reynolds Lewis, K. (July/August 2015). What If Everything You Knew About Disciplining Kids Was Wrong? Retrieved http://*www.motherjones.*

com/politics/2015/05/schools-behavior-discipline-collaborative-proac-tive-solutions-ross-greene.

Chapter 8

Okun, MD, M. S. (February 2014). Dopamine Pumps for Parkinson Disease: Has the Time Come? *Lancet Neurology*.
http://www.jwatch.org/na33446/2014/02/04/dopamine-pumps-parkinson-disease-has-time-come.

Ferenczi, E., & Deisseroth, K. (2016). Illuminating next-generation brain therapies. *Nature Neuroscience*. http://web.stanford.edu/group/dlab/media/papers/ferencziNatureNV2016.

Zhang, F., Wang, L. P., Brauner, M., Liwald, J. F., Kay, K., Watzke, N., . . . Deisseroth, K. (5 April 2007). Multimodal fast optical interrogation of neural circuitry. *Nature*. doi:10.1038/nature05744.

George, M. S., Taylor, J. J., & Short, E. B. (2013). The expanding evidence base for rTMS treatment of depression. *Current Opinions in Psychiatry*. 26(1), 13-18.

Sackeim, H. A., Prudic, J., Fuller, R., Keilp, J., Lavori, P. W., & Olfson, M. (January 2007). The cognitive effects of electroconvulsive therapy in community settings. *Neuropsychopharmacology*. 32(1), 244-254.

George, M. S., Sackeim, H. A., Rush, A. H., Marangell, L. B., Nahas, Z., Husain, M. M., . . . Ballenger, J. C. (15 February 2000). Vagus nerve stimulation: a new tool for brain research and therapy. *Biological Psychiatry*. 47(4), 287-295.

Michael, L., Rohan, R. T., Yamamoto, C. T., Ravichandran, K. R., Cayetano, O. G., Morales, D. P., ...Paul, S. M. (November 2013). Rapid Mood-Elevating Effects of Low Field Magnetic Stimulation in Depression. *Biological Psychiatry.* 76(3), 186-193.

Chapter 9
Writer, Gazzaley, MD, PhD, A., & Director, Brown, E. (March 5, 2013). *The Distracted Mind.* Santa Fe Productions, Inc. PBS Distribution. [DVD].

Abbott, A. (September 4, 2013). Gaming improves multitasking skills. *Nature News.* Nature Pub.

Hamilton, J. (September 2013). *Multitasking after 60: Video Game Boosts Focus, Mental Agility.* National Public Radio.

Test of Variables of Attention, TOVA. Retrieved www.tova.com.

Chapter 10
Weil MD, A. (1972). *The Natural Mind: A New Way of Looking at Drugs and the Higher Consciousness.* Boston, MA: Houghton Mifflin.

Weil MD, A. (2007). *Eight Weeks to Optimum Health: A Proven Program for Taking Full Advantage of Your Body's Natural Healing Power.* (Rev. Ed.). New York, NY: Ballantine Books.

Chbosky, S. (February 1999) *The Perks of Being a Wallflower.* New York City, NY: Pocket Books.

Chapter 11

Clark, D. A., & Radomsky, A. S. (2014). Introduction: A global perspective on unwanted intrusive thoughts. *Journal of Obsessive-Compulsive and Related Disorders.* doi:10.1016/j.jocrd.2014.02.001. Retrieved http://www.sciencedirect.com/science/article/pii/S2211364914000128.

Greenberg, PsyD, J. L., Wilhelm, PhD, S., Feusner, MD, J., Phillips, MD K. A., & Szymanski, PhD, J. (2016). Cognitive behavioral therapy (CBT) has been shown to be helpful in treating BDD symptoms both in individual therapy or in group therapy, and is the only type of psychological treatment for BDD that is supported by research. *OCD Foundation.* Retrieved https://bdd.iocdf.org/about-bdd/

Phillips, MD, K., Wilhelm, Dr. S., & Steketee, Dr. G. (2013). *Cognitive-Behavioral Therapy for Body Dysmorphic Disorder: A Treatment Manual.* New York, NY: Guilford Press.

Pallanti, S., Grassi, G., Sarrecchia, E. D., Cantisani, A., & Pellegrini, M. (2011). Obsessive–Compulsive Disorder Comorbidity: Clinical Assessment and Therapeutic Implications. *Frontiers in Psychiatry.* 2(70). Retrieved http://doi.org/10.3389/fpsyt.2011.00070.

Baer, L., Jenike, M.A., & Minichiello, W. E. (1986). *Obsessive Compulsive Disorders: Theory and Management.* Littleton, MA: PSG Publishing.

Jenike MD, M. A. (2001 Winter). An update on obsessive-compulsive disorder. *Bull Menninger Clin.* 65(1): 4-25. Review. PMID: 11280957.

Blair Simpson, MD, PhD, H., Foa, PhD, E. (11 September 2013). Exposure/Ritual Prevention Therapy Boosts Antidepressant Treatment of OCD. *JAMA.* Retrieved http://www.nimh.nih.gov/news/science-news/2013.

Harris, R. (1 November 2009).
ACT Made Simple: An Easy-To-Read Primer on Acceptance and Commitment Therapy. Oakland, CA: New Harbinger Publications.

Jenike, Dr. M., & Zine, E. (2 April 2009).
Life in Rewind: The Story of a Young Courageous Man Who Persevered Over OCD and the Harvard Doctor Who Broke All the Rules to Help Him. New York, NY: HarperCollins.

Phillips, K. A. (February 2004). Body dysmorphic disorder: recognizing and treating imagined ugliness. *World Psychiatry.* 3(1), 12-17. Retrieved http://www.ncbi.nlm.nih.gov/pmc/articles/
PMC1414653/

Feusner, J. D., Neziroglu, F., Wilhelm, S., Mancusi, L., & Bohon, C. (2010). What Causes BDD: Research Findings and a Proposed Model. *Psychiatric Annals.* 40(7), 349-355.

Chapter 12

Sederer, Dr. L. (15 April 2013). *A Family Guide to Mental Health Care.* New York, NY: W. W. Norton & Company.

Health Insurance Portability and Accountability Act, HIPAA, a US law designed to provide privacy standards to protect patients' medical records and other health information provided to health plans, doctors, hospitals and other health care providers. Retrieved http://www.hhs.gov/hipaa/for-professionals/privacy/laws

Sederer, L. I., & Sharfstein, S. S. (2014). Fixing the Troubled Mental Health System. *JAMA.* 312(12), 1195. doi:10.1001/jama.2014.10369.

Chapter 13

Kabat-Zinn, Dr. J. (24 September 2013).
Full Catastrophe Living: Using the Wisdom of Your Body and Mind to Face Stress, Pain, and Illness. (Rev. Ed.). New York, NY: Bantam.

Winston, D., & Smalley, Dr. S. (13 July 2010). *Fully Present: The Science, Art, and Practice of Mindfulness*. Boston, MA: Da Capo Lifelong Books.

Kabat-Zinn, Dr. J. (6 February 2010). *Wherever You Go, There You Are: Mindfulness*. New York, NY: Hachette Books.

Kabat-Zinn, Dr. J. Mindfulness Meditation: What It Is, What It Isn't, And It's Role In Health Care and Medicine In: Haruki, Y., Ishii, Y., and Suzuki, M. *Comparative and Psychological Study on Meditation*. Eburon, Netherlands, 1996. Pg. 161-169.

Van Halen. (1991). Right Now. [Recorded by Van Halen] *For Unlawful Carnal Knowledge*. [CD]. Burbank, CA: Warner Brothers Records. Sony/ATV Music Publishing LLC, Warner/Chappell Music, Inc., Universal Music Publishing Group.

Epilogue

Rothschild, Dr. A. (Ed). (2 December 2011). *The Evidenced-Based Guide to Antidepressant Medication*. Arlington, VA: American Psychiatric Publishing.

American Psychiatric Association. (27 May 2013). *Diagnostic and Statistical Manual of Mental Disorders (DSM)*. *(5th ed.)*. Arlington, VA: American Psychiatric Publishing. Major Depressive Disorder (MDD).

ABOUT THE AUTHOR

F. D. Raphael built a career in the music industry, working for the David Geffen Company, Aerosmith, Rhino Entertainment, Concord Music Group, and Bertelsmann Music Group in a wide range of creative and executive roles. She executive produced the critically acclaimed theatrical release *DeRailroaded: The Wild Man Fischer Story*, a film about Fischer's colorful music career and the paranoia induced by his manic-depressive schizophrenia.

Raphael graduated from Rutgers University with a BA with honors in English and Mass Communication. She interned for legendary publisher William Phillips of *The Partisan Review* and attended the Writer's Program at Bennington College before becoming a staff writer for *The Middlesex Daily News* in Massachusetts.

In 2011, Raphael received the prestigious California State Parent Teacher Association Honorary Service Award. She works with UCLA's Depression

Grand Challenge Advocacy Team and lives in Los Angeles, California, with her husband and their dogs, Foster and Posse 2. They have two grown sons.

Cover art by the author's son. *Portrait on a Napkin,* circa 2006

INDEX

Made in the USA
Charleston, SC
28 August 2016